LIBRARY MANUALS

Volume 2

COMMERCIAL AND TECHNICAL LIBRARIES

COMMERCIAL AND TECHNICAL LIBRARIES

J.P. LAMB

LONDON AND NEW YORK

First published in 1955 by George Allen & Unwin Ltd

This edition first published in 2022
by Routledge
4 Park Square, Milton Park, Abingdon, Oxon OX14 4RN

and by Routledge
605 Third Avenue, New York, NY 10017

Routledge is an imprint of the Taylor & Francis Group, an informa business

Copyright © 1955 by Taylor & Francis.

All rights reserved. No part of this book may be reprinted or reproduced or utilised in any form or by any electronic, mechanical, or other means, now known or hereafter invented, including photocopying and recording, or in any information storage or retrieval system, without permission in writing from the publishers.

Trademark notice: Product or corporate names may be trademarks or registered trademarks, and are used only for identification and explanation without intent to infringe.

British Library Cataloguing in Publication Data
A catalogue record for this book is available from the British Library

ISBN: 978-1-03-213109-2 (Set)
ISBN: 978-1-00-322771-7 (Set) (ebk)
ISBN: 978-1-03-213167-2 (Volume 2) (hbk)
ISBN: 978-1-03-213169-6 (Volume 2) (pbk)
ISBN: 978-1-00-322797-7 (Volume 2) (ebk)

DOI: 10.4324/9781003227977

Publisher's Note
The publisher has gone to great lengths to ensure the quality of this reprint but points out that some imperfections in the original copies may be apparent.

Disclaimer
The publisher has made every effort to trace copyright holders and would welcome correspondence from those they have been unable to trace.

COMMERCIAL AND TECHNICAL LIBRARIES

BY J. P. LAMB

City Librarian, Sheffield

WITH A PREFACE BY
SIR WALTER BENTON JONES, BART
M.A., LL.D.
Chairman of The United Steel Companies

LONDON
GEORGE ALLEN & UNWIN LTD
& THE LIBRARY ASSOCIATION

First Published in 1955

This book is copyright under the Berne Convention. Apart from any fair dealing for the purposes of private study, research, criticism or review, as permitted under the Copyright Act 1911, no portion may be reproduced by any process without written permission. Enquiry should be made to the publisher.

© *George Allen & Unwin Ltd , 1955*

*in 12pt. Old Face Special type by
C. Tinling & Co., Ltd.,
Liverpool, London and Prescot*

TO SIR HENRY GREGORY
K.C.M.G., C.B.

*with whom I was privileged to
be associated in a difficult but
agreeable task*

Commercial Library, Glasgow. [*frontispiece*

GENERAL INTRODUCTION TO THE SERIES

The publication of a systematic series of authoritative Manuals of Library Work, which shall survey Library polity and practice in their latest aspects, is a requirement of which administrators, librarians and students have long been conscious, and is much overdue.

The Library Act of 1919 marked the end of one long epoch and the beginning of a new. The removal of the rate limit paved the way for remarkable extensions and innovations, both in buildings and service. The great work of the Carnegie Trustees in fostering the development of urban Public Libraries has been largely diverted into fresh channels, and County Library Systems now cover the country from Land's End to John o' Groats. The public demand for, and the appreciation of, Libraries have increased enormously. The evolution of Commercial and Technical Libraries and the development of Business and Works Libraries would amply suffice to indicate this progress, but, during the last decade or so, the entire field of Library service has been subjected to review and experiment, and little, in administration or routine, remains unchanged.

It will, therefore, be obvious that old textbooks on practice can no longer serve, and there is need for new manuals, written by persons of experience and authority, and treating of the new conditions in a full and practical manner. These Manuals are designed to fill the void, and the fact that they are issued by Messrs. George Allen and Unwin Ltd., in conjunction with the Library Association, should afford adequate proof of the qualifications of the authors to treat of the subjects upon which they will write.

GENERAL INTRODUCTION

The volumes will be supplied with bibliographical references throughout, and will be illustrated when necessary. No effort will be spared to make the series an essential tool for all those who are engaged in Library work, or who intend to embrace Librarianship as a profession.

WILLIAM E. DOUBLEDAY
General Editor until 1949

To Mr. Doubleday's general introduction, written more than twenty years ago, it need only be added that the plan and purpose of these Manuals remain unchanged.

DUNCAN GRAY
General Editor

PREFACE

As we grow older we fall into a way of quoting our forebears to illustrate their superiority or our degradation. My father, who was trained as a mining engineer, once told me that when he was learning his profession he set as his target the knowledge and the practice necessary to sink and equip a mine in the middle of the Sahara desert without the assistance of any other expert in his profession or in any other profession.

I do not know whether Mr. Lamb consciously set himself a target of this kind and I would hesitate to refer to the ground on which he had to work as a desert. But in the library world he has been a pioneer. He was not content to supply the needs of those who read for leisure or learning; he set himself to provide every kind of information for those who seek it in the workaday world of industry and commerce.

And now he has added to his own literary achievements this manual in which it is possible to read not only how to design, build, equip and staff a library, but how to conduct it for the benefit of all sorts and conditions of men.

It is a great pleasure to contribute a preface to this work. It is written as a manual and as such it is complete. But as I read it I see as others will see a striking picture of the lifework of an enthusiast who has succeeded in putting into practice so many inventions, so much practical experience, so much of himself. The edifice and organization which he has created is a monument to the city in which he lives and an example which in future many will choose to follow.

In the mind of the common man a library is a repository for books and a public library is a place in which are kept

PREFACE

a greater variety of books and information than he can keep himself or borrow from his friends and which he can read at will. Research he connects with chemical laboratories reserved for the use of strange men. He does not know how wide a field is covered by research, still less does he realise that research and books go hand in hand. Most research establishments whether large or small have their own libraries. But few can be large enough, and in these days the largest public libraries have organized special libraries of commerce and industry which not only augment the information of research establishments but are available to individuals or firms too small to justify a library of their own.

The Science and Commerce departments of Public Libraries do more than provide books of reference; they have staffs especially trained to provide information. In the South Yorkshire industrial area the Sheffield Science and Commerce Library answers thousands of enquiries of a highly specialist character from the library's own resources. And the service goes further than answering enquiries. For twenty years it has administered an Interchange Organization in exchanging knowledge of industrial experience which rarely gets into print. Regular contacts made in this way build up a community of friends which breaks down barriers and substitutes enlightened cooperation.

All these services have given and are giving great help to the industries of Sheffield and, as I know well, to my own firm. We are all grateful for the services and we are grateful to those who administer them. The development of similar services in all industrial areas surrounding our great cities would not only be a benefit to them but might lead to the building up of a still larger reservoir of technical experience and a wider exchange of information. It is good to know that firms all over the country are creating

PREFACE

libraries to advance research and study among their staffs. This book will be a help to them. It tells of the problems they will have to meet. It makes clear that there is more in the task than the collecting of books and statistics. The need to select books and information with judgment, to train staff to interpret them and to choose men with natural gifts for their work, all these needs and others are described and emphasised in the following pages, and it is interesting to mark how like they are to the needs of every constructive occupation.

Mr. Lamb treats each branch of his subject clearly and thoroughly. He is convinced that invention and discovery are needed more than ever if we are to survive as an industrial nation. If we are to supply these needs, he says, we must regard our sources of information as no less important than our workshops and pay no less attention to them.

His book is convincing and full of interest. As a manual it will be read by librarians. As an instructive and entertaining story about libraries, books and information, and their blood relationship with invention and enterprise, I commend it both to librarians and industrialists.

Walter Benton Jones

The United Steel Company Limited
17, Westbourne Road
Sheffield, 10
24th August, 1954

AUTHOR'S FOREWORD

This work deals only with British public commercial and technical libraries. Many details of methods in general use have been excluded because librarians administering such departments have plenty of experience in applying accepted library practices adequately dealt with in text-books. For somewhat similar reasons, complete lists of books, periodicals and sources are not included. In the existing state of publishing—particularly of periodicals—many references would have become outdated almost immediately; moreover, other books have so excellently covered some fields that it would be an impertinence on my part to attempt to emulate them. These deliberate limitations of the book's scope have allowed certain principles to be discussed at some length without imposing too much print on colleagues already staggering under the amount produced by more facile pens. As for its other shortcomings, I can only plead that a busy librarian, who puts the efficiency of his libraries before all things, suffers from the handicap of lack of time, apart from any more grievous natural disabilities.

For anything worth while in this work I am indebted to colleagues in other cities and towns who uncomplainingly completed, and later revised, a questionnaire of such terrifying length and detail that it might well have been devised in one of the newer ministries, and to many closer colleagues in the Sheffield City Libraries who have contributed their considerable gifts to its making. Not least among the debts I owe them is the pleasure of hearing, in the friendly yet critical atmosphere of our discussions, how far removed from their conception of what such a book

AUTHOR'S FOREWORD

should be is the one I now submit to a profession which, though it should have become inured to the worst that writing librarians can impose on it, is asked to face still another trial.

CONTENTS

GENERAL INTRODUCTION TO THE SERIES	page 7
PREFACE	9
AUTHOR'S FOREWORD	13
I. *History*	19
II. *General Principles*	55
III. *Plan and Furniture*	72
IV. *Staff*	101
V. *Book Stock*	125
VI. *Patents and Trade Marks*	173
VII. *Organisation and Administration*	192
VIII. *External Activities*	234
IX. *The Future*	269
INDEX	311

ILLUSTRATIONS

Commercial Library, Glasgow	*frontispiece*
	facing page
Directory shelves with reading slope—Science and Commerce Library, Sheffield	96
Sheffield Science and Commerce Library—training students from the College of Commerce in the use of business books	97
Commercial Reference Library, Liverpool	224
Commercial Library and Information Department, Manchester	225
Technical Library, Manchester	225
Scientific and Technical Section—Science and Commerce Library, Sheffield	240
Science and Commerce Library, Sheffield	241

CHAPTER 1

HISTORY

THOUGH special departments of commerce and technology in public libraries have a comparatively short history, a proposal for the formation of a mercantile library in the City of London was made as early as 1754. In that year, an unknown writer suggested[1] that "as there is now found to be more Room [in the Mansion House] than the Lord Mayors have need of, a convenient apartment be allotted for a publick Mercantile Library, to be consulted by all the Citizens, as occasion may require". Nothing came of this proposal, though the author offered to bequeath his own extensive collection of mercantile books and papers for the purpose, and tried to arouse the City's pride by pointing out that "as such a Publick Repository of mercantile knowledge would be the first of its kind probably in all Europe, it would be therefore the more worthy of the first Commercial City in the Universe".

The subject was raised again in the *Report from the Select Committee on Public Libraries*, 1849, in which

[1] "An Essay on the Many Advantages accruing to the Community from the Superior neatness, &c., of Great and Capital Cities, particularly Apply'd to the City and Suburbs of London, the renowned Capital of the British Empire, addressed to Sir John Barnard, Knt., Senior Alderman and Senior Representative in Parliament of the said City", London, 1754.

COMMERCIAL AND TECHNICAL LIBRARIES

it is stated: "Special libraries would no doubt form themselves in appropriate localities. At Hamburgh the commercial library has been famous for more than a century. Its existence is stated by Dr. Meyer to have had a most beneficial influence on the character of the merchants of Hamburgh. It would seem that in our large commercial and manufacturing towns, as well as in our agricultural districts, such libraries would naturally spring up, illustrative of the peculiar trade, manufactures and agriculture of the place, and greatly favourable to the practical development of the science of political economy".[1] Some of the evidence given before the Committee shows a surprisingly modern outlook on the value of both commercial and technical libraries, though the latter were considered only in relation to local manufactures. Some members of the Committee were clearly envisaging libraries of commerce and industry as alternatives to general public libraries, but the Committee agreed that, even if general libraries were established, the maritime cities, such as Liverpool, Glasgow, Hull and Bristol, should provide libraries of commerce, and Manchester and Leeds should naturally stock books dealing with the cotton and woollen trades respectively. Such libraries, the Committee stated, "would produce great advantages, not only in imparting general instruction, but also in promoting the extension of the commerce and manufacture of the town".[2]

[1] *Report from the Select Committee on Public Libraries*, 1849, p. xi.
[2] Op. cit., p. 140.

HISTORY

In 1869, Dr. W. Sedgwick Saunders, who was the prime mover in the reconstruction of the Guildhall Library, included among his six suggestions the provision of a "library of reference free to all respectable persons desirous of making temporary use of dictionaries, maps, plans, works upon commerce, banking, etc." From the inception of the new library in 1873, the Guildhall Library has included a collection of books, directories, codes, manuals and trade papers useful to those wanting business information.

Apart from the City of London, which, as the centre of the country's finance and commerce, naturally gave early attention to the provision of sources of commercial information, and Manchester, where the Library Committee minuted a resolution in 1852 to the effect that one of the objects of the reference library should be to collect books on trade and commerce, there is no evidence that public library committees showed any interest in the development of commercial or technical libraries until the turn of the century. There were several reasons for this. The Select Committee's recommendation of a "small rate" and its belief that libraries could be built up by gifts of books, handicapped the work of all libraries in the early years of the movement. Many of the arguments advanced in favour of general libraries were based on moral and social grounds, and library committees, when they were empowered in 1855 to buy books, gave preference to works which met a general demand. The nation's commerce and industry were developed without serious

COMMERCIAL AND TECHNICAL LIBRARIES

opposition from other countries until towards the close of the century; a world eager for goods bought readily from almost the sole producer. At a time when there was a general belief that Britain, as the "workshop of the world", could always maintain that privileged position, there was no real incentive to organised research, either in commercial methods or industrial processes. The literature of commerce and industry was therefore not large, nor was any considerable demand for it apparent, except in the case of simple text-books for the artisan. The public library was moulded on the tradition of the Mechanics' Institute. In an age of rugged individualism, with a rapidly increasing and largely illiterate urban population, those hungry for education seized upon the many "self-educators", whilst many a great industry was founded by hard-working men whose inspiration was Samuel Smiles and the simple text-book, and whose university was the public library.

The steady march of prosperity of the country began to slow down towards the end of the century. In the keener competition of those years, science was more and more applied to industrial needs. The literature of commerce and industry grew with the demand for information.[1] Many towns had removed the shackles of the rate limitation through local Acts of Parliament, and began to provide books on those

[1] The reader is referred to E. Wyndham Hulme's important study of the growth of scientific and technical literature: "Statistical bibliography in relation to the growth of modern civilisation", 1923.

HISTORY

subjects in increasing numbers; they followed the normal practice of catering for the needs of their readers so far as their means allowed. The town library usually had an "open shelf" collection of directories, annuals, and other quick reference books of a commercial type, and included in the reference library technical dictionaries and a reasonable range of books and periodicals dealing with local industries. In the large cities, where the demand was greater, these collections were more up to date, and were often of considerable size. But the idea of creating special libraries to deal with commercial and technical subjects only, with separate staffs who could undertake the work of indexing and abstracting, and could become experts in these limited fields, only began to be voiced in any volume during the war years of 1914-1918. The technical developments forced on this country by war conditions made clear the need for research. This, in turn, drew attention to the lack of facilities for research in the form of technical libraries of a new type; whilst the virtual cessation of foreign trade made thinking men realise that only an intense concentration on marketing and other commercial problems would make it possible for much of the lost trade to be regained.

As early as 1901 Mr. L. Stanley Jast had pointed out the need for expanding the provision of technical books in public libraries, and suggested that the technical collection should include, in addition to reference books and text-books, monographs, the transactions of societies, and magazines. "If the

COMMERCIAL AND TECHNICAL LIBRARIES

technical library is to be of real service it must be kept up to date. It must have the latest books, and it must have the latest editions of the books it has."[1] Some recognition of, and assistance to, the work of public libraries had been given as a result of the passing of the Technical Instruction Act of 1889, and the Local Taxation (Customs and Excise) Act of 1890. By this second Act, a portion of the Excise Duty had been assigned to local authorities to be expended on technical education or in relief of the rates, at their option. "In most cases the windfall was expended on what was ostensibly technical education; but so liberally was that term interpreted that it was made to cover well-nigh every branch of knowledge, Latin and Greek excepted; and the Science and Art Department by its money grants supported the interpretation."[2] Twenty-six public libraries were receiving such contributions, commonly known as "whisky money", in 1902, and in some towns the annual grant had been considerable; the first year's grant to Liverpool, for example, was £1,500, but by 1902 it had dwindled to £250.

This unexpected generosity was not extended to public libraries because local authorities had suddenly recognised their value; it came because the Technical Instruction Act of 1889 ignored the School Boards. The local authorities, with no experience in educational work and no administrative machinery

---

[1] Jast, L. Stanley. "Technical libraries." *Library World.* Vol. 3, 1900-1, p. 259.
[2] Adamson, J. W. *English education,* 1789-1902, 1930, p. 410.

HISTORY

to carry it out, suddenly found themselves with an embarrassment of riches in the form of whisky money, which had to be expended in conformity with the Act. The provision of technical literature in public libraries was one way of doing it.

The Education Act of 1902 contained provisions which affected the continuance of these grants. The Local Education Authority replaced the School Board, and technical education became part of Higher Education; and the grants from Excise Duties were made available for these wider activities. Public libraries lost the whisky money not because there was any legal restriction on the use of it for their benefit, but because the newly-created educational authorities found plenty of scope for using it for what they considered to be more strictly educational purposes.

The position of public libraries in relation to technical education was discussed at the Annual Meeting of the Library Association held at Leeds in September, 1903, at a conference on "The relations between public education and public libraries" to which prominent educationalists had been invited. The following resolution was passed: "That this meeting of librarians, members of library committees and delegates from secondary education bodies recognises the creation of a technical library in every technical educational centre as an essential of any well-considered scheme of technical education, and believes that the best way of providing such libraries is by the technical education authorities making grants from the special funds at their disposal to the public library authority in each district."[1]

It is not clear whether at this time the idea of a separate library which would allow the staff to give a specialised service had been considered, though the importance of the "trained administration which the public library provides"[2] was recognised. The number of technical books published in this country was small, and compared unfavourably with the output of other countries.[3]

The main concern of librarians was to provide technical books in greater numbers than had hitherto been possible, and to house and administer them in the public library rather than in the technical college. It was claimed, in support of the suggestion, that the public library served a wider adult public, was free from the limitations of class teaching, and could bring to the organisation of such libraries special technique, a trained staff, and the wide resources of the general stock of books.

The time was not ripe for any considerable development of library activities in special fields, and the few efforts of librarians to arouse interest in the provision of technical literature met with no response until 1907, when the Manchester Chamber of Commerce moved in the matter. The chamber prepared a report showing comparative figures of

[1] *Library Association Record*, 1903, p. 494.
[2] Jast, L. Stanley. "Technical libraries." *Library Association Record*, 1903, p. 469.
[3] Op. cit., p. 472.

HISTORY

book stocks, costs, etc., of the Manchester Reference Library, the Patent Office Library, and certain American public libraries, in support of a suggestion made to the Manchester Libraries Committee that it was desirable to have a technical library as part of the city's service.[1] It was not until the 1914–18 war had been in progress long enough to show the extent of the country's technical deficiencies that the matter was raised again at a meeting of the Society of Chemical Industry, in 1915, when a resolution "that the establishment of technical libraries is of urgent national importance" was passed unanimously.

Though there was a stronger and more conspicuous demand for technical libraries, the commercial type was the first to be established in Britain. Mr. Robert Adams, Assistant City Librarian of Glasgow, made the first detailed proposal for the creation of a special commercial library as part of the municipal library service in the larger centres of population, in a paper read before the Scottish Library Association in June, 1913. The suggestions of Mr. Adams were of considerable importance in influencing the development of the Glasgow Commercial Library and other libraries which later drew on Glasgow's experience. He outlined in detail the nature of the material such a library should contain, the organisation of the service, and the type of staff required.

[1] It is interesting to note that this report was used again when an influential deputation representing many societies put similar views forward in 1918. See page 39.

COMMERCIAL AND TECHNICAL LIBRARIES

He stressed the need for intelligent, highly-trained librarians, who would be expert researchers, and the importance of speedy service. The Libraries Committee of the Glasgow Corporation began to examine the question of establishing a library for business men in October, 1913, but for various reasons consideration of the proposal was postponed, and the outbreak of war further delayed matters. It was not until the 3rd of November, 1916, that this commercial library was opened in premises readily accessible to the business community, and it is pleasing to record that due credit for the inauguration of the movement was paid to Mr. Adams by the Chairman at the opening ceremony.

As the Glasgow Commercial Library was the first of its type to be established in Britain, and its experience helped those authorities which later followed Glasgow's example, a brief description of its contents and methods may not be out of place here. The material provided included 100 directories, atlases, maps, codes, telephone directories and telegraphic addresses, suitable government publications, manufacturers' and trade catalogues (an arrangement for the loan of any of the 10,000 foreign trade catalogues collected by the Commercial Intelligence Branch of the Board of Trade was also made), standard business reference books, reports of chambers of commerce and trade associations, and 100 periodicals. Patents were also available in this library. The following records were prepared by the staff: a classified card register of business firms, a

HISTORY

register of translators (eleven languages were already represented when the library was opened), and a register of printers in foreign languages.

The Glasgow Libraries Committee wisely placed this new venture in premises which could readily be extended should the use of the department call for more accommodation for readers and books. As the initial stock of books was small, arrangements were made to draw books as required from the general library stocks by means of a twice-daily motor delivery service. The assistance of business firms in the city was solicited in many ways, and it was stated that "the desire of the Committee is to obtain experience as to the best lines upon which this new undertaking might be effectively and successfully developed".

From now on the interest in commercial and technical libraries grew rapidly, not only among librarians, but in governmental, commercial, scientific and industrial circles. The complacency of British commercial and industrial life was greatly disturbed during the war years, and there seems little doubt that one of the main reasons for the strong desire for the establishment of commercial—and later, technical—libraries, was a recognition of the truth that in a competitive world the best equipped nation wins, and that the hitherto unchallenged supremacy of British commerce and industry had been seriously undermined by the zeal of energetic competitive nations. It was further realised that whatever the result of the struggle might be in a military sense, conditions at the end of the war would make a rebuilding of commercial and industrial life imperative, as the concentration of the country's energies on the prosecution of the war had resulted in the neglect of markets held for generations. "One of the essentials to success in the coming competition for the markets of the world is that reliable information should be immediately available when required, and in this connection a well equipped and efficient commercial library and bureau might render invaluable assistance."[1]

In the year that the commercial library was opened, representatives of fourteen scientific and technical societies and institutions met in Glasgow on the 27th June, to discuss methods of pooling scientific and technical literature. A committee was formed to undertake the production of joint catalogues of technical books in the libraries represented at the meeting. The Public Libraries Committee later gave its support, and Mr. S. A. Pitt, the City Librarian, joined the committee and acted as editor. The cost of production was borne by contributions from all the participants, and arrangements were made for students to consult any of the books required in the society and institutional libraries. Three lists only were published at considerable intervals:—*Aeronautics* (July, 1917); *Internal Combustion Engines* (February, 1918); *Motor Vehicles* (October, 1922).

[1] Pitt, S. A. *The purpose, equipment and methods of the Commercial Library*, Glasgow, p. 8.

HISTORY

Liverpool followed the example of Glasgow by opening a commercial reference library in the Exchange buildings, the business centre of the city, on 1st August, 1917. The special sub-committee of the Public Libraries Committee appointed to undertake the formation of this library co-opted representatives of the Chamber of Commerce and five important trade associations. Some of these bodies gave practical help as well as expert advice, presenting books, reports and periodicals, and assisting in the collection of other material. The library was well housed in a large room, easily accessible, by its three entrances, to members of the various exchanges adjacent to it and the staffs of the great business, banking and insurance offices which cluster in that part of the city. It opened with a stock of 3,000 books and 250 periodicals, and in view of the city's great maritime trade and tradition, the collection of maps was very extensive even in the earliest days. In 1939 it was moved to similar and spacious premises in the rebuilt Exchange.

Meanwhile, the Library Association had begun to interest itself in these matters. In August, 1916, on the proposition of Mr. E. A. Savage, it asked the Committee of the Privy Council for Scientific and Industrial Research whether that Committee would be prepared to receive evidence from the Library Association on the subject of the establishment of technical libraries throughout the country, and in October, after an interview with Sir William McCormick, Chairman of the Advisory Council, formed a special committee of eleven members to prepare a report on the means of strengthening the technical departments of public libraries. At its first meeting the Committee asked that its terms of reference should include commercial libraries, and that it should be known as the Technical and Commercial Libraries Special Committee. Work was immediately begun on a series of far-reaching enquiries, and the activities of the Committee were of such importance in furthering the establishment of special libraries that they are described in some detail in this chapter.

A *Report on Trade Catalogues* was approved in March, 1917. It dealt with the purpose, methods of collection, administration, binding and shelving of trade catalogues and recommended that, in view of the special difficulties inherent in the methods of collecting and organising them, and in order to obtain the widest dissemination of the valuable information they contain, proposals be submitted to the leading professional societies and trade journals for standardisation of production and possibly for the publication of periodical condensed catalogues of British firms. For this purpose it was urged that trade catalogue literature should be surveyed and classified, and that committees representative of each class should be appointed to advise on the publication of their sections. The Committee recognised that only a body of experts could settle the type of catalogue best suited to a particular class of industries. It therefore merely drew attention to the chaotic state of trade catalogue publication in this country, and

HISTORY

offered to co-operate in any efforts made to standardise it.

A further *Report on Patent Libraries* was published shortly afterwards, and an attempt was made to compile a directory of patent publications supplementary to that appearing in the *Illustrated Official Journal (patents)*.

The Committee, through the Library Association Council, issued an *Interim Report on the provision of Technical and Commercial Libraries* which was submitted to the Annual Meeting of the Association in October, 1917. In this report it was stated that the Council had laid a memorandum before the Department of Scientific and Industrial Research, advocating (a) the removal of the rate limit, (b) a closer union between state and copyright libraries and municipal libraries in order that the resources of the former should be indirectly available for scientific and technical students in the provinces, and (c) government grants to some State supported library for the purchase of books required for research, such books to be available for loan to public libraries. The memorandum was supported by statistics of scientific and technical book provision in public libraries. Some of the details quoted by Mr. E. A. Savage in the discussion on technical libraries at the 1917 Annual Meeting make sorry reading. It seems quite clear that the majority of public libraries were at that time unable to provide even the quantity of books required, and though the question of quality or up-to-dateness was not mentioned, there can be

COMMERCIAL AND TECHNICAL LIBRARIES

little doubt that many of these books would be quite useless, if not positively harmful, to students.

Though the recommendations to the Department of Scientific and Industrial Research were the most important part of this report, in that they were designed to influence the policy of the Government on libraries, other recommendations were included on scientific and technical libraries, commercial libraries, and their relations with government departments and the training of special librarians. They are summarised below:—

Scientific and Technical Libraries

It is of urgent national importance to increase the supply of scientific and technical books and periodicals, the existing supply being quite inadequate for higher research and in many places insufficient for the requirements of the student and the citizen. It is strongly urged, therefore, that:

(a) local authorities should afford more generous support to public libraries for the provision of scientific and technical literature.

(b) municipal and other libraries should co-operate in issuing union catalogues of technical books and adopt such other co-operative methods as will make their resources available over a wider area.

(c) a State scientific or technical library should publish periodically a descriptive list of selected books in Science and Technology.

(d) a more extended use should be made of periodical literature by the increased provision of current indexes and digests.

HISTORY

Commercial Libraries

It is possible, in the library of every trade centre, to form special sections which will provide business men and others with much information valuable to them in business. The practice has been to store books useful to business men with the general collection. The Council recommend that, wherever possible, these collections be brought together to form special libraries, as in Glasgow and Liverpool. Such a library should include:—

> Commercial and Industrial data (Governmental reports, parliamentary publications relating to commerce, trade periodicals and catalogues, reports of Chambers of Commerce, statistical publications).
>
> Geographical information (atlases, maps, gazetteers, directories).
>
> Transport and communication (shipping, railway and postal guides, telephone directories, telegraphic codes).
>
> Financial information (tariffs, foreign exchanges, banking, company reports).
>
> Commercial and Industrial Law.
>
> Business Organisation (office methods, advertising, salesmanship, works management, accountancy, etc.).
>
> Working collection of general and special reference books.
>
> Journals of Commerce, Industry and Finance.

In libraries where it may not be practicable to establish separate commercial libraries, printed catalogues of business books would serve a very useful purpose.

Relations with Government Departments

The Board of Trade Commercial Intelligence Branch

COMMERCIAL AND TECHNICAL LIBRARIES

should send all official publications on commerce to provincial libraries as soon as published and free of cost.

Items from the collection of foreign trade catalogues made by this department should be lent to public libraries on request. A better plan would be for the Department to obtain additional copies and send these to public Commercial Libraries.

The Council are glad to note that the defects in publishing commercial information collected by the Consular Service, Board of Trade Commercial Intelligence Branch, the scientific and technical staff of the Imperial Institute and the Agencies General for the Colonies have been considered and proposals for their reform are in course of being carried out.

Training of Special Librarians

The Council are of opinion that the possession of scientific and technical qualifications will not itself suffice unless the holder has previously received the foundation of a sound library training. A special librarian is one with a special knowledge of the literature of his subject and of the way to organise it for use, and not necessarily one with a special knowledge of the subject itself.

The question as to what steps should be taken to provide research material for commercial and technical students and workers had become of national importance in 1917. It was known that the Government had made a grant of a million pounds to the Committee of the Privy Council for Scientific and Industrial Research, and as some of this would probably be spent on libraries and books, the Library Association attempted to ensure that the existing organisation provided by public libraries, however inadequate their technical books provision was at that time, should not be overlooked, Faced with rising costs through war conditions, the majority of public libraries were finding it difficult to give reasonable service, and the steep rise in prices during the next few years made their task even more formidable; the rate limitation became an intolerable burden. The efforts of public librarians to obtain government recognition of their work had a double purpose: they wished to obtain financial assistance for special libraries, and the removal of the rate limit by legislation was constantly in their minds. Library Association activity during 1917 and 1918 was dominated by a desire to attain these ends.

At the 1917 Annual Meeting of the Library Association considerable time was given to discussions on commercial and technical libraries. The conference was attended by many influential persons, including the Minister of Reconstruction (The Right Hon. Dr. C. Addison, M.P.), who touched on libraries of commerce and industry in his address. Resolutions urging the formation of municipal commercial and technical libraries in all important centres were unanimously adopted after discussions which kept to a consistently high level. The resolution on commercial libraries suggested that they should act as branches of the Commercial Intelligence Department of the Board of Trade.

Copies of these resolutions were sent to the Minister of Reconstruction, the Board of Trade Intelligence Department, and the Department of

COMMERCIAL AND TECHNICAL LIBRARIES

Scientific and Industrial Research, with requests that they would receive deputations from the Library Association. A further resolution asking the Board of Trade to supply free to all libraries establishing commercial collections copies of consular reports, and other government publications containing information useful to business men, was agreed to by the Board, which undertook to send copies of its publications to such commercial libraries as were in a position to make full use of them. The Board, however, doubted whether it would be practicable to constitute such libraries official branches of the department.

It was then suggested that the Technical and Commercial Libraries Special Committee should take steps to bring its work to the notice of technical societies, and that more representatives of science and industry and fewer librarians should serve on it. The first of these suggestions was acted on, and the Interim Report was submitted to the Institution of Civil Engineers, the British Engineers' Association, the Institution of Automobile Engineers, the Society of Chemical Industry, and the Manchester Engineers' Club and other local bodies.

This Committee subsequently spent much of its time in considering the formation of a Technical and Commercial Libraries Section of the Library Association. Although its desirability was stressed on many occasions, and draft bye-laws were prepared, such a section was never actually formed.

In the meantime, the efforts of 1917 began to

HISTORY

show results in a growing interest in the provision of technical libraries. Public libraries were now pressing for the establishment of technical libraries in the larger industrial towns and the creation of a national lending library of scientific and technical books to supplement their work. Apart from the value of such a national library as a book and periodical reservoir, it was hoped that its staff could publish a bibliography and a periodical index to scientific literature, and assist librarians in the choice of books. Later in the year, the Manchester Engineers' Club passed a resolution affirming the necessity of a technical department of the municipal library, and requesting the Libraries Committee to make such a provision. Similar resolutions were subsequently passed by nine other societies in Manchester. A deputation from them interviewed the Libraries Committee, and advocated the formation of a Manchester District and National Technical Library, supported in part from national funds and serving more than a purely local purpose.

Industrialists and scientific workers were also considering this matter in their own associations, though from a somewhat different angle. Sir Robert Hadfield, F.R.S., had called attention in April, 1918, to the poor facilities possessed by research and technical societies, large and small, for carrying on their work. The best use of scientific knowledge and its application to industrial and commercial needs could not be made unless there were facilities for meetings and adequate library accommodation. He sug-

COMMERCIAL AND TECHNICAL LIBRARIES

gested the provision of a single building for the various technical societies, in which there must be a library equipped with tens of thousands of books and papers now required by those studying technical developments.[1]

The Faraday Society later discussed the co-ordination of scientific publications; in the course of the meeting Mr. Savage's suggestion of a central library and bureau of information came in for attention.[2] It was felt that expense would be a difficult obstacle, and that some means of linking up existing libraries would be the ultimate solution. It is interesting to note that the need for expert staff was recognised at this meeting. Mr. Michael Longridge, the President of the Institution of Mechanical Engineers, suggested the formation of a College of Librarians, where a body of men, well educated and well paid, would keep track of papers read and researches in progress, so that enquirers could be told where to get the information they required.

The discussions on the provision of technical information which were being carried on at this time in scientific and industrial circles showed that while a considerable volume of informed opinion favoured a central co-ordinating bureau, the idea of amalgamating the libraries or other activities of existing societies would not be likely to receive much

---

[1] See p. 287 for details of governmental plans for carrying out this suggestion.
[2] "The co-ordination of scientific publication," *The Engineer*, Vol. 125, 1918, pp. 402–404.

HISTORY

support. Sir Robert Hadfield pointed out that feeling was even against the suggestion that the younger institutions should be merged as branches into the older ones. "There is a distinct desire to preserve the individuality of the various institutions, and the formation of new ones, as fresh branches of science manifest themselves, would apparently not be regarded unfavourably."[1]

Scientific workers were, however, aware that there was much overlapping. Its extent could be seen in the duplication of work done by the societies, as shown in the papers read at meetings and in the publication and indexing of scientific papers. The view that this work should be handed over to a central body, such as the Conjoint Board of Scientific Societies, which had been formed in 1916 to consider the matter, met with some approval. Mr. J. G. Pearce, F.R.S., however, suggested that the Library Association, in conjunction with the leading scientific and engineering institutions, should form a permanent central body of trained workers from schools of library science, who would systematically classify, index and abstract scientific information.[2] Mr. Pearce clearly had in view the linking up of existing libraries and research organisations by the central clearing house, and he pointed out that such an organisation would provide a single channel by which foreign information could reach this country;

[1] *The Engineer*, Vol. 125, 1918, p. 402.
[2] Pearce, J. G. "The future of documentation," *Library Association Record*, 1918, pp. 162–166.

moreover, it would be able to arrange and secure the acceptance of a standard system of classification, publish a union list of periodicals, and possibly print catalogue cards of articles in the more important periodicals for rapid distribution.

A further move to enlist the help of industry in the library campaign was made at a conference of the North Central Branch of the Library Association at Manchester on 23rd–24th October, 1918. Representatives of fifteen commercial, technical and other associations attended, and two papers were given on technical libraries by men engaged in industry. Mr. R. H. Clayton[1] supported the idea of creating a number of large and well-equipped libraries in the chief industrial centres, maintained partly by grants from the Committee for Scientific and Industrial Research, partly by the municipalities, and partly by subscriptions from private firms. Mr. J. G. Pearce also advocated State assistance, but differed in regard to the location, and to some extent the scope, of such libraries. He pointed out that scientific literature was daily becoming increasingly subdivided, and the literature in any branch would therefore appeal to a smaller number of workers. There was a limit to the extent to which local funds could properly be applied to the purchase of specialised scientific books in a variety of branches of research, but the possibilities of success would be greater if technical libraries were located according to specialisation or concentration of

[1]Clayton, R. H. "The public technical library," *Library Association Record*, 1919, pp. 5–8.

HISTORY

industries. Thus Manchester might specialise in textiles; Sheffield in steel; Birmingham in non-ferrous metals; Leeds in wool, etc., and these libraries should be in constant telephonic and postal communication. There were many excellent suggestions in this thoughtful address,[1] particularly in regard to the co-operation between works and public libraries in book stocks, administration methods, and interchange of staff. Some of them are, in fact, being carried out to-day.

A resolution passed at this conference advocated the establishment of fully equipped and intensively organised technical and commercial libraries under municipal control in the half-dozen chief industrial centres, to be aided by government grants, these large district libraries to be related to the smaller technical collections in their vicinity.

Towards the end of 1918 the Technical and Commercial Libraries Special Committee urged the continuation, after the war, of the *Technical and Economic Supplements* to the *Daily Review* of the foreign press which had been issued by the War Office since the early part of the year. The War Office had established in 1917 a Technical Information Service, primarily for military purposes, and intended for technical specialists in the various government departments, but as the periodical review of technical literature which it published became more widely known and increasingly demanded, it was placed on

[1]Pearce, J. G. "The works library and its relation to the public technical library," *Library Association Record*, 1919, pp. 8–12.

sale. The basis for this publication was a general Engineering Index on cards, in which the compilers attempted to include every item of engineering information published throughout the world. This service formed, in fact, a Department of Technical Intelligence of an extensive kind, and the War Office gave careful consideration to the possibility of continuing this service after the conclusion of hostilities, preferably in co-operation with libraries and research societies. The Library Association Committee supported the suggestion that the Technical Information Service be constituted an independent body on the lines of the British Engineering Standards Association, and stated that, in its view, the essential features of a successful information service were (a) close co-operation between societies and journals publishing abstracts, to prevent overlapping and to avoid the dispersal of bibliographical material, (b) frequent publication of the general index, (c) amalgamation of the libraries of the chief technical societies, (d) the foundation of a national lending library of applied science, and (e) the co-operative use of photo-copying processes.

As a result of the success of the Manchester conference, the Library Association suggested that similar conferences should be held in Birmingham and Glasgow, and an afternoon session of a one-day conference was given to commercial and technical libraries on the 2nd May, 1919, at Birmingham. A resolution similar to that approved at Manchester was passed unanimously.

HISTORY

The Library Association had now accepted the principle of government grants being made to half a dozen libraries, which would be selected according to their position in the centre of large industrial population groups. Such libraries would be general technical libraries, linked up with the smaller technical libraries in the area, and performing, for these areas, much the same functions as the Patent Office Library was doing for London. These libraries in turn would draw on a national technical collection, which would also be assisted by government grants.

But the Department of Scientific and Industrial Research, which had been created in 1916 to administer the decisions of the Committee of the Privy Council, had moved along different lines. Research associations had already been formed by certain of the chief industries, and were being assisted by grants, mainly on a pound for pound basis, from the Department. The draft Memorandum of Association for these bodies issued by the Department in 1917 included as one of their objects the formation of libraries and the collection of statistics and information relating to the industries. The use of these libraries and the bureaux of information which it was assumed would naturally develop from them was to be confined to the members; since the existence of the research associations depended on the sums received from firms engaged in the industries, it was clearly impossible to make these services freely available. Public librarians strongly opposed the principle that information collected partly at

COMMERCIAL AND TECHNICAL LIBRARIES

the expense of the State should be used for the benefit of research associations alone.

Despite the efforts of the Library Association under the active and able leadership of Mr. E. A. Savage, the Adult Education Committee of the Ministry of Reconstruction, which issued its eagerly awaited report on libraries and museums on the 1st of May, 1919, was no more helpful than the Committee of the Privy Council for Scientific and Industrial Research in regard to the claim that the commercial and technical departments of public libraries should receive government recognition. The general tenor of the recommendations is summed up by the following sentence which appears early in the report: "In the case of general libraries the unit of organisation and administration is the local authority, in the case of the technical library system it should be the industry."[1] The influence of the findings of the Committee for Scientific and Industrial Research, which are quoted extensively by the Adult Education Committee, is apparent. The Committee pointed out the importance of public libraries containing an adequate supply of books dealing with the various trades of the district, but argued that a comprehensive policy of technical library provision must be organised industry by industry, and it should clearly be closely related both to technical education and research.

The Committee recognised that public libraries

[1] Ministry of Reconstruction. *Third Interim Report of the Adult Education Committee: Libraries and Museums*, 1919, p. 10.

would naturally provide literature dealing with predominant local industries, but as they could not be expected to purchase costly technical works of an advanced type for which there would only be a relatively small demand, or books on industries of little local importance, their stocks would have to be reinforced from other sources. Demands which could not be met by the public library should be satisfied by libraries which the Committee suggested should be organised by the industries.

The Committee therefore proposed that each industry should make a survey of its library facilities, including the libraries of universities, technical colleges and institutes, and professional associations. If this survey showed that the provision of literature in existing libraries was adequate to supply normal needs, the problem was one of mobilising these resources and making them available; where the supply was inadequate, it would be necessary to establish a national library for the industry concerned or perhaps for a group of allied trades. A central library organisation for each industry would be necessary in any case.

It will be seen that the Committee had in view a national or central library organisation for each industry, the size and work of this library depending on the extent of the existing provision of technical literature from all other sources.

The function of each of these central or national industrial libraries would be to supplement the book stocks of existing libraries; and to act as a medium for the exchange of books among them. The library should contain the results of recent research, at home and abroad, foreign technical works, complete files of British and foreign trade journals and relevant official publications of this and other countries. Such a library might become an Intelligence Department for the industry and should work in close touch with the research association. To cover the cost of capital outlay and maintenance, the Committee recommended that a state grant not exceeding 25 per cent. of the sums received from other sources should be made.

The public library had a very limited place in this scheme. It was expected to supply literature to cover the less specialised needs of local industries and of certain diffused trades, such as building, bakery, etc., and presumably, had these proposals been adopted, to co-operate with the central libraries of the industries with which its work was related. The stocks of the central libraries of industries and their outlier libraries would be supplemented by a central circulating library—a development of the Central Library for Students.

In dealing with commercial libraries, the Committee did not consider the degree of specialisation envisaged for technical libraries to be necessary, as the function of the commercial department of the local library was primarily to provide books concerned with commercial subjects, rather than detailed information on matters of trade.

The report of the Adult Education Committee

HISTORY

was a bitter blow to the hopes public librarians had cherished of government recognition of their work.[1] The Committee's findings included some of the suggestions put forward by the Library Association, but there was little evidence of any recognition of, or belief in, the service the public library could offer to industry; on the contrary, the Committee (in its reference to commercial libraries particularly) suggested that there should be limitations to that work.[2] The Committee's attitude to the technical sections of public libraries is perhaps not surprising in view of the obvious limitations of the service at that time. All the available evidence—some of it advanced by librarians at their meetings, to support the plea for the abolition of the rate limit—showed that library book stocks generally were insufficient and largely out of date. But such criticisms could not justly be made of commercial libraries, as two of them had been established long enough to prove their value; their work was, in fact, constantly being extended. It seems clear that the Library Association had not been able to educate public opinion sufficiently in regard to the potentialities of the public library service. The library movement failed to obtain recognition, not because of inherent defects,

[1] A detailed summary of the report, by Mr. E. A. Savage, will be found in the *Library Association Record*, 1919, pp. 154–159.
[2] Mr. E. A. Savage severely criticised the report in a paper read at the 1919 Conference of the Library Association. "Technical libraries: a comment on the third Interim Report of the Adult Education Committee." *Library Association Record*, 1919, pp. 264–270.

but largely because of a statutory financial limitation, the harmful effects of which, as prices advanced during the war years, became increasingly apparent.

Almost the last action of the Library Association's Technical and Commercial Libraries Special Committee was to draft a memorandum on the report of the Adult Education Committee for submission to the President of the Board of Education. This memorandum was issued in September, 1919. In it the Library Association offered a reasoned criticism of certain recommendations, and finally stressed the following points:—

1. No steps had been taken by the Committee for Scientific and Industrial Research to ensure the provision of technical literature.

2. A general technical library, under one administration and with all necessary facilities for the distribution to any industry of books required, would be immeasurably better than scattered collections, housed in different places, inconvenient to outside users, and disproportionately costly.

3. The greatest value of the report of the Adult Education Committee lay in its recognition of the need for mobilising scattered resources and its proposals for a central circulating library.

The work of the Technical and Commercial Libraries Special Committee has been dealt with in some detail because it has some relevance to present day tendencies and at the time was of the utmost value in stimulating the interest of library authorities. It could not have been without considerable

HISTORY

influence on the Government's policy towards libraries; and the passing of the Libraries Act of 1919 which, by abolishing the rate limit, made possible an expansion of library activity far greater than any special grants for limited purposes could have done, was probably helped by the vigorous and intelligent activities of the Special Committee. When national feeling was stirred by the technical deficiencies exposed by war needs,[1] the Committee wisely seized every opportunity of stressing the importance of the contribution public libraries could make to the provision of technical literature, and its many activities had the dual merit of being at once practical and wide ranging. Its work ceased in 1919, and in 1922 it was not reappointed.

Meanwhile, the first joint commercial and technical library had been opened in Leeds in July, 1918. A commercial library formed in 1915 at Coventry was placed in a separate room in 1917-18, and others

[1] The case of optical glass was the outstanding example of the country's partial dependence on enemy industry. The important literature on the subject was in German, and no translations were available. In 1916 the Committee of the Privy Council for Scientific and Industrial Research authorised the issue in revised versions in English of L. O. M. von Rohr's "Die Theorie der optischen Instrumente, I Band. Die Bilderzeugung in optischen Instrumenten vom Standpunkte der geometrischen Optik" (issued in 1920), A. Gleichen's "Die Theorie der modernen optischen Instrumente" (issued in 1918), and "Die Fundamental-Eigenschaften der dioptrischen Instrumente: elementare Darstellung der Gauss' schen Theorie und ihre Anwendung", the German version of G. Farraris's "Le proprietà cardinali degli strumenti diottrici" (issued in 1919). All were to be sold at cost price.

COMMERCIAL AND TECHNICAL LIBRARIES

were created in Dundee, Wolverhampton, Birmingham and Manchester in 1919. Bristol followed in 1920 with its library of commerce, and Sheffield, like Leeds, organised a joint commercial and technical library. The development of technical libraries was more leisurely. Coventry opened a technical library in July, 1918,[1] Manchester in 1922, and Birmingham in 1924. Edinburgh waited until 1932 before providing a commercial library, while a joint commercial and technical library was formed in Leicester in 1936. The only pre-war separate commercial library in London was opened in a branch of the Southwark Public Libraries in 1937.

Both Manchester and Sheffield made changes in the organisation of their special libraries when new central library buildings were opened in both cities in 1934. The commercial library of Manchester, which had been housed in the Royal Exchange, was combined with the technical library on the first floor of the new building. In 1937 a further regrouping of the central library departments was undertaken, involving some important changes in the administration of the commercial and technical libraries. The commercial library was moved to the ground floor as a quick reference library. The main stock of books on commerce, and the whole of the technical library were transferred to the reference library. Ten years

[1] Excellent book lists on such subjects as "Technical chemistry", "Aeronautics", "Metallurgy", "Aluminium and its alloys", "Works management", "Oxyacetylene and electric welding and cutting", "Science and the crafts", were issued in Coventry between 1916 and 1919.

later, a rearrangement of the central library departments allowed the creation of an extended library of science and technology with adequate accommodation for books and readers.

The accommodation for the commercial and technical library was more than doubled in the new building in Sheffield. The stock of the technical library was increased by the transfer of books on pure science from the reference library. Though they are housed in two wings of one room, have a joint catalogue and are administered by the same staff from a central point, the commercial and the scientific and technical sections are distinct as regards book stock, periodicals and readers. The joint library has now been renamed the Science and Commerce Library.

Other libraries greatly extended their collections of books and material dealing with commerce and industry. As early as 1924 it was recorded that there were commercial collections in 46, and industrial collections in 70, libraries.[1] Though the number and quality of books and periodicals naturally vary, there can be no doubt that public library authorities in general accept their responsibilities to readers who require information on commercial and industrial matters.

The research libraries provided by the various industries through their research associations have grown in number and importance since the policy

[1] Board of Education. Public Libraries Committee. *Report on Public Libraries in England and Wales*, 1927, p. 128.

COMMERCIAL AND TECHNICAL LIBRARIES

of organising scientific and technical research by industries was adopted and partly financed by the Department of Scientific and Industrial Research. These and other special libraries formed The Association of Special Libraries and Information Bureaux (ASLIB) in September, 1924.

The national awakening of interest in scientific and technical research which followed the First World War has been eclipsed by that resulting from the Second and its late by-product, nuclear fission; with this is linked a general recognition of the need to rebuild the nation's economic life by encouraging the study of ways of increasing industrial efficiency. The reports and recommendations of the government committees which have been considering these matters are dealt with in the last chapter. Meanwhile, progress in the formation of special departments in public libraries has continued. New commercial and technical libraries were opened in Hull and Newcastle-upon-Tyne in 1951. Liverpool, already notable for the efficiency of its commercial department, created a technical library in 1952 to cater for the needs of its newly-established industries, and Holborn, the second metropolitan borough to provide a special service, organised a commercial library in 1953. In the following year the pioneer commercial library of Glasgow was transferred to the spacious and dignified Royal Exchange building.

CHAPTER II

GENERAL PRINCIPLES

THE creation of special departments of commerce and technology in public libraries can only be justified if a sufficient need exists, or can be presumed to exist, for their services. Its extent is determined by two factors: the number and importance of the commercial and industrial activities in the area, and the presence of a large body of scientific and technical students, considerations which are often mutually inclusive. A department providing specialised literature and a trained staff, and in which advanced study and research are carried out, is really only required in cities where there is a large enough concentration of trade and industry to offer some guarantee that the use of its services will justify the cost of establishment and maintenance.

Smaller places have, of course, their own problems. It is obvious that the library finances of a small town are not generally sufficient to support such a library under existing conditions of local rating, nor would the number of specialist or advanced students likely to use it make it worth while even if the money were forthcoming. On the other hand, there are towns where technical interests are large in proportion to the size of the population, such as one in which the buildings of a regional technical college are situated, or one which (like Rugby) is dominated by a single industry. In those cases a special library, if provided, would probably justify itself by use, but would be open to criticism on the ground that the money spent on it had been unfairly diverted from the services to the general reader. The public library committee could reasonably suggest that it was the responsibility of the education authority or the industry to serve its own needs; the public library, on its part, would continue to shelve adequate stocks of general technical books in the home reading department for the use of all grades of workers, just as it normally caters for other professional and technical readers. Such problems are outside the scope of this work, which is primarily concerned with the kind of department to be found only in the large library systems; even they must examine the number, range and type of industrial and commercial undertakings they can serve and decide, on the merits of the case, whether the conditions in their own area really make such provision necessary.

The populations of the towns which have established special departments vary from 240,000 to over a million, with the exception of one town of 167,000 people, where it is to be presumed that exceptional reasons governed the decision to create one. In London, the Cities of London and Westminster have impressive collections of commercial material, and two metropolitan boroughs, Southwark and Holborn, have separate commercial depart-

GENERAL PRINCIPLES

ments; but there are no special technical libraries of the kind found in the large provincial cities. The concentration of bibliographical material of all kinds in London makes it unnecessary for any public library there to attempt to make full provision for the research worker in special fields, as it could not acquire the resources of the national, research association, society, trade, and other special libraries in the metropolis, to which the reader usually has access through his membership of professional or other societies.

Existence of other libraries

In the large centres, which are usually focal points for contiguous populations, there are various types of special libraries whose existence must affect the work of the commercial and technical library and even the principles on which it is founded and organised. They comprise those of universities, chambers of commerce, colleges of commerce and technology, research associations, industrial research libraries founded by individual firms or groups of firms and some institutes or societies usually concerned with certain industries of a localised kind.

As most of these libraries are private, and limit their service to their members, or are established to serve a restricted clientèle in temporary association with them, the public library, which exists for the general body of citizens, has no choice but to provide a service which may partially duplicate one already in existence. Many chambers of commerce, for example, have good libraries and excellent information services; but being maintained by the subscriptions of members, who might be tempted to relinquish their membership if some of its privileges could be obtained without payment, they cannot act as public services without risk to their income. Moreover, the cost of administration would be increased if their activities were extended, even partially, to new users. Society and works libraries are in the same position. The case of those university libraries which have special library departments is somewhat different, as they share in the grants from the University Grants Committee, while the provincial universities also receive substantial annual sums from the municipal and county authorities in their areas. It would seem reasonable to suggest that in return for this support from national and local public funds the universities should be required to extend their library services, under certain specified conditions, beyond their own students and staffs. The libraries of the colleges of commerce and technology might also be encouraged to accept a wider responsibility than that of providing large and well-equipped libraries for use only by those receiving instruction there.

The linking up of many types of libraries through the Regional Library schemes and the National Central Library and its outliers, has shown what voluntary library co-operation can achieve in bringing books to readers who need them. The general acceptance of this co-operative principle has made it possible for the special libraries in an area to evolve forms of joint service which, if properly organised, may ultimately increase the efficiency of all of them by avoiding unnecessary duplication of those books and services which meet important but limited needs. It would be unreasonable to expect private libraries to throw open their doors to the general body of students, but they are usually willing to lend books to the public library, and in some cases to accept readers recommended by it. The public library is, of course, available to their members. The existence of such libraries, and their willingness to collaborate with the public library, will therefore have an important effect on the range of the book stock and the form of the service offered by commercial and technical libraries.

Populous urban areas

In most cases these factors will be valid for a district as well as a town. The civic authorities of cities situated in the midst of a large urban industrial area, or which, because of their size and importance or their historical position, are the natural centres to which near-by populations turn for what may be called provincial metropolitan services, usually conceive it to be their duty, or in their interests, to consider the needs of the surrounding area when planning their library activities. Their reference libraries are freely used by many people who live outside their borders; some allow the use of the lending libraries to non-citizens on equal terms with their own ratepayers; and most of them offer at least partial borrowing rights to persons employed or being educated within their boundaries. The provision of special libraries in such cities is, therefore, conditioned to some extent by the requirements of surrounding populations as well as by those of their own citizens, and the service given is wider than that of a more isolated town which, because of its geographical position, need only plan with local needs in mind.

Changed conditions of technical research

It has been pointed out that commercial and technical libraries were first created during the war of 1914–18, when the provision of information on these subjects was found to be inadequate. Public librarians urged that if such libraries were organised in the largest centres of population and were aided by State grants and a national lending library service, they would be able to serve fully the needs of commerce and industry. These views were not accepted, and subsequent developments make it unlikely that they ever will be. Since then, and particularly during recent years, there has been a remarkable acceleration in the volume and pace of research and its application to industrial processes, which has brought into being many agencies designed to provide the means for such research. The number of trade and industrial research associations is now considerable; they have been able, through their well-trained staffs of scientists and their well-stocked

GENERAL PRINCIPLES

libraries, to help in the development of old industries and the creation of new ones. Technical processes have become increasingly sub-divided, and laboratories and libraries have followed the trend. For workers in advanced fields the general technical library can only have a limited usefulness, and the vast output of printed matter is far too great for any but a special library to attempt to collect it. Inevitably the need for the co-ordination of the sources of scientific and technical information has become a paramount consideration in all research establishments, and many agencies, chief among them the Department of Scientific and Industrial Research, have made various essays in this direction. These will be dealt with later. The point to be kept in mind at this juncture is that the commercial and technical library cannot work in isolation if it is to do its job properly: it becomes a part of a great and rapidly growing organisation designed to provide the research worker with any detail he needs from the world-wide network of scientific and technical information now available.

Effect on public libraries

Even when a separate technical department of the public library is created, it is unlikely to be able to provide from its own resources material for advanced research, unless the industries are largely uniform or are connected with one product. It would hardly be possible for the library authority of a city with hundreds of different trades to acquire all the detailed literature dealing with them if it happened to be extensive in all or even in most cases. Librarians, however, have always had to face the problem of selecting what they need from the enormous mass of printed matter available, and the difficulty being general, means have been devised for its solution by the publication of union lists (such as the *World List of Scientific Periodicals*), abstracts and indexes, and by the general willingness of all libraries to exchange their material. It is usual for the technical library to provide adequate literature on the industries of its district so as to serve the general student or enquirer, but to rely on national systems of book and periodical exchange for material which will satisfy the less common enquiry and the needs of the specialist. It should, of course, attempt a degree of specialisation in the literature relating to certain industries of primary importance to the town's economy.

The need for a special library

The business man and the research worker both need accurate information quickly. If it is not accurate, the business man may lose financially and the technical research worker may reach false conclusions, which may result in production waste, or, at the least, in waste of time. The business man, basing a quotation on information received from a library on such matters as tariffs, dock and harbour dues, freightage costs, etc., may suffer serious financial loss if the information is inaccurate. The technician is less likely to err, because the service he usually asks for is the production of sources of information which his knowledge and training enable him to check.

The organisation and work of the special library of commerce and technology must, therefore, be based on two main general principles: its stock must be up to date and extensive enough to meet the demands of most of its users, and the staff work must be highly efficient.

It would be difficult, if not impossible, for a librarian working in a general library to give competent service of so specialised a kind. The range of information contained in books is so wide that, even if sources of information only are asked for, the general reference library assistant could hardly obtain sufficient experience and knowledge of this one department of research to be able to find them even with the aid of an extensive range of bibliographical tools. The majority of students who use general reference libraries have some experience in the use of libraries and books, but the commercial and technical library will attract many readers who need a great deal of help and guidance. In the commercial library particularly, the librarian will often find it necessary to obtain the actual information for the enquirer, for many business men are strangely unaware of the value and importance of books in their job, and the commercial colleges, like the schools, rarely include courses of bibliographical training in their curricula. The librarian must therefore specialise. By limiting his work to commercial and technical matters he is able to acquire an extensive knowledge of the material he uses and the needs of those who consult him; and he can use this knowledge effectively in the organisation and direction of his department. His experience equips him to give better personal service, and to create useful indexes, analytical catalogues, clippings files and other essential aids to the provision of accurate information.

Good results can certainly be achieved in a general library by arranging for some members of the staff to be responsible for dealing with commercial and technical enquiries and for the selection and maintenance of books and other records in these sections. Some libraries do, in fact, give useful service to commerce and industry in this way without creating a special department. But where the demand is considerable, a separate library has definite advantages. It has already been shown that special libraries are only properly effective in the larger cities and towns. Their general reference libraries are so large that only a small proportion of the total stock can be consulted by readers at the shelves, and though there may be an excellent catalogue, the unskilled library user may miss much useful material. By separating from the main stock books, periodicals and other matter concerned with commerce and industry and shelving them in a room where most, or perhaps all of them, can be seen and readily used, the reader is helped in many ways. The shelves are not encumbered with books outside the range of his special interests; he can link up his study of textbooks with current information in periodicals and in society and other publications; and he has the use of indexes, abstracts, files and other library records specifically designed to meet established needs in limited fields of knowledge. Not least in importance are the personal contacts which result from the separation of readers and staff from the main body of library activity.

The type of library

The nature of the economic life of a town will indicate the type of special library it is desirable to create. The seaport cities of Glasgow and Bristol have active commercial libraries, each varying in the type of service it offers according to the needs of its users. Birmingham and Manchester, with thriving and extensive industries and wide commercial interests, have formed separate libraries for commerce and for technology. Liverpool, which has a highly developed commercial library in the heart of the business and shipping area, has met the demands of new industries attracted to the city by forming a technical library, for which spacious quarters are planned in the proposed reconstruction of the "blitzed" portion of the central library buildings. In other towns, the two libraries are run jointly, emphasis being laid on the one or the other according to the district's requirements and the use of the library. Leeds and Sheffield, for example, find it convenient to merge them. In Leeds, a commercial centre of some importance, the service of the joint library is about equally balanced between commerce and industry. The "producing" city of Sheffield places the emphasis on the technical side of its work, and is fortunate, from a library point of view, in that the industry of the city itself and the surrounding district is almost wholly concerned with the production and working of special alloy steels and ancillary products, so that a degree of specialisation rarely possible in a public library is attained. These examples emphasise the importance of making a careful survey of the relative value of the town's commercial and industrial activities, and in certain cases of those of the adjacent districts, before it is decided what kind of special library should be organised. The only effective test, however, is experience of the needs of readers as shown by the use of the library; and it may be that the original conception will be modified or expanded as the service develops.

Location

The commercial library may serve two purposes: to give an information service to the business man while he is engaged in the conduct of his affairs, and to act as a reference library of commerce for the student.

It is a generally accepted principle that the commercial library should be easily accessible to the business community. Where the main library building is reasonably near the commercial centre—assuming that any particular part of a city can be so described—there are obvious advantages in housing all library departments in one building, where every kind of book and record is quickly available; but if the main library is some distance from the business area (or has no suitable accommodation) it will probably be thought advisable to acquire or rent premises more conveniently placed for the business man. The commercial library, in this case, would primarily be a commercial information library; its books, periodicals and other material would be selected, and its organisation designed, with that end in view. The needs of the student would be met in the general reference library of the main building.

Though the principle of ready accessibility may at first sight appear to be attractive, further consideration suggests that premises separated from the main library should be only provided in exceptional circumstances. The business quarter of most large cities covers a wide area, and only a small proportion of those who work in it can be within immediate reach of the library, wherever it is placed. Every office cannot have a library beside it, and if an enquiry is of sufficient importance, it is reasonable to expect the firm concerned to instruct a responsible member of the staff to go to the library to make it and take some trouble to obtain the right answer. Moreover, many enquiries can be dealt with by telephone, though this is not an unmixed blessing, since it transfers work from the reader to the staff. It is noteworthy that the telephone is being increasingly used, even for enquiries which are by no means easy to answer, and this is creating serious staffing problems.

COMMERCIAL AND TECHNICAL LIBRARIES

The cost of providing the large premises required in the heart of the commercial quarter is so considerable that few authorities could entertain it. Probably the best position for a commercial information library is in one of the exchange buildings. Experience shows, however, that it may be improperly used if placed there. People find it a convenient room in which to meet, as it is well known and open for long periods; unless it is strictly controlled, it may be used as a rent-free office by the business touts who frequent the centres of commerce; and even the most tactful librarian may find it difficult to decide at what point certain uses of the library have ceased to be legitimate. It is interesting to note that these difficulties were taken into account when the Manchester Libraries Committee decided to transfer the commercial library from the Royal Exchange to the new central library.

Another serious objection to separate premises is that there must always be occasions when material needed either at the commercial library or the main library is stocked at the other. Most of these difficulties can be overcome by duplicating certain books, by the use of the telephone, or by a regular system of messengers; but all these methods are wasteful, and are not entirely effective. Further, as the student of commerce and collateral subjects will be catered for in the general reference library, he will lack there the help of those members of the staff who are thoroughly conversant with the current needs and problems of commercial life.

GENERAL PRINCIPLES

The advantages of unified administration in one building are considerable, and are not lightly to be disregarded; unless there are exceptional circumstances they will probably be found to outweigh the arguments for creating a commercial library in separate premises.

This applies with even greater force to the technical library because of the nature of its organisation and service. As its users are scattered, the actual position of the library—provided it is reasonably central—is not of importance, since industrial establishments, even in those cities which are fortunate enough to have confined their industries to one or more districts, are almost as widely spread as the homes of those who work in them.

The technical library stock, too, covers a wider range of subjects than the commercial library, and study of these subjects so often impinges on ideas, experiences and practices outside the special library's scope that the student may find it necessary to refer to books in the main library stock. Conversely, the reader in a general reference library frequently wishes to use the technical library. It is not possible, even if many books are duplicated, to make the technical library and the general reference library each completely self-contained; and if the technical library is housed in a separate building away from the main library, delay in supplying information and books is inevitable. The technical library should therefore be placed in the main library if there is suitable accommodation.

COMMERCIAL AND TECHNICAL LIBRARIES

A joint commercial and technical library is usually provided when there is not sufficient use of the books and material on either commerce or technology alone to justify the cost of administration of two separate establishments. In these circumstances there appears to be little point in placing a joint library in the business quarter, as part of its service is intended for a different type of user. Joint libraries are usually found in the smaller cities, where the library resources are not so strong, and where there is a correspondingly greater need for linking up the stock and service with those of the general library.

In practice, the main library buildings of most cities in this country are sufficiently central to make this question a somewhat academic one. The grouping of commercial and industrial firms in large units strengthens the arguments for housing the special departments in the main library building. The administrative and research staffs of great industrial combines are now often housed in offices and laboratories in the suburbs of our cities. As they administer industries scattered over a wide area, there is no reason why the headquarters staffs should be adjacent to one or other of the works, but there are many reasons why they should have the advantage of the light, quiet and cleanliness offered by the residential suburbs. The general commercial institutions—the banks, insurance, shipping, export and other mercantile offices—will probably continue to cluster in central areas.

GENERAL PRINCIPLES

Differences in practice

The traditional conception of a library as being primarily concerned with preserving books has made it difficult for librarians of general libraries to realise how much their functions have been changed by the great increase in the number of books dealing with practical subjects and matters which by their nature can only be of topical interest; but the special libraries provided for sections of the community whose main preoccupation is with the necessities of trade were naturally freed from any such limitations. From the beginning, those who gave thought to their organisation brought to the task an objectivity of mind which can usually only be achieved where there are no precedents to canalise thought. It was rightly insisted, for example, that use is the determining factor in book choice, and this alone is so complete a break with tradition as to be worthy of note. The work and development of commercial and technical libraries rested on empirical methods from which certain principles of organisation soon emerged; and later experience has proved these to be so sound that they have hardly changed since the first of them began its work.

CHAPTER III

PLAN AND FURNITURE

As most commercial and technical libraries have been organised in rooms adapted for the purpose in existing buildings, they offer little guidance to those planning a new central library in which the department is to find a place; and the difficulty of laying down any general principles is increased by the fact that practices vary greatly in different towns and are reflected in layout and furnishing. The commercial and technical library is one of many departments, and must conform to the general architectural scheme; even its position in the building is governed by factors which must be balanced against the needs of the other departmental libraries. Nevertheless, a brief review of certain building details which the librarian and his committee must bear in mind may not be out of place here, though they will be applicable to the building as a whole, rather than to a part of it.

While the value of a library depends primarily on the quality of its contents and the efficiency of its staff, the physical conditions under which it is administered are not without influence on the library's effectiveness. The importance of good planning, which will provide suitable comfort for readers, give them ready access to the books and periodicals, and allow the staff to provide a speedy and competent service, should not be underrated. Excellent work has been and is being done in inadequate buildings with makeshift furniture, and this is sometimes urged as a reason why change is unnecessary, particularly if it involves considerable expense, as it is almost bound to do. The experience of one of the two cities where new central libraries have been built suggests that a properly planned and equipped department both helps the reader and allows the staff to do their work more effectively, for though no major changes in the organisation of the commercial and technical library were made, its work has increased very greatly since it was removed to premises properly planned and furnished for the purpose.

Both branches of the department have somewhat similar problems. They must cater for two kinds of user—the casual reader who uses the enquiry service, quick reference books, or periodicals, and the student who may work for long periods on lines of study or research requiring a high degree of concentration and mental effort. While the former is not unduly troubled by noise or movement, the serious student needs conditions which give him comfort and quiet. Good natural and artificial light, sensible, convenient and comfortable furniture, easy accessibility of books and service, a layout plan which prevents unnecessary contacts between casual and serious book users, are all desirable. The well-planned library is a result of a rational balancing of all these considerations with the type of service it is designed to give.

PLAN

The size of the public part of the library must be based on the number of books it is thought necessary to have on open access and the estimated peak attendance of readers. In making this estimate, due allowance should be made for the fact that as most of the large number of periodicals provided are published on the last days of the week, an exceptionally large influx of readers may be anticipated on these days. An area of 1,500 feet super is suggested as a minimum for the public room, apart from stack, workrooms, filing rooms, etc. If a smaller room has to be used, some material which properly belongs to it must be shelved elsewhere, and the library's efficiency suffers.

The type of plan most favoured is one in which the shelves are placed around the walls, the centre being kept clear of bookstacks or high fittings, and furnished with various kinds of desks, tables, or special fittings, for reading and for using maps and plans. Complete oversight is useful as a check against theft of books or parts of them (a serious problem during the book-starved war years) and it also helps the staff to offer immediate service to a reader who appears to be in difficulty. The service point should be sited so as to allow the staff to control the entrance and yet be readily accessible to readers both when they enter the library and when they are working in it.

Though there are practical reasons why wall

shelving is preferable to island bookcases, it has one disadvantage if, as is often the case in a departmental library in a central building, the only natural light comes from side windows above the shelves along one side of the room. If the window light is strong, the reader using books below them finds it difficult to read their titles. Many factors affect the degree of nuisance this causes: the height of the windows themselves, the distance between the window bottom and the top of the shelves, and the existence of windows in other walls. Roof lighting gives the best kind of natural lighting, particularly in a library with wall shelving, but this can rarely be provided in a composite library building. When there are side windows only they should be placed as high as possible, and never less than 6' 6 from the floor, so as to give an uninterrupted run of wall shelving space. Low windows give additional light and add to the room's appearance, but they occupy valuable wall space and are sometimes used by readers to watch happenings outside the library. Moreover, as the shelving has to be fitted round them, it increases the cost considerably. Whenever possible, there should be windows in more than one wall; their cross light helps the reader using the wall shelves. These matters are subject to the architect's calculations of the amount of window space required to give adequate natural light to the room. The accepted relation between window height and the width of the room must be observed; if it is not, the whole room, as well as the wall shelves, may be inadequately lit. The librarian should call the architect's attention to all the considerations involved and ask him to make his plan and design his elevation accordingly.

Constant weeding of outdated books from the open shelves is essential, but there can be little objection to as large a number of books as possible being placed on open access in this type of library, because, apart from the special quick reference sections, its users are mostly special students who should be able to use a large classified stock without difficulty. If space permits, alcoves might well be made by projecting double-sided bookcases from the wall shelving, preferably at the end of the room farthest from the entrance, provided that there are windows in that wall. These afford quietness and "atmosphere" for readers engaged in close study. If this is done, it may be thought desirable to break the classification sequence and shelve in the alcoves runs of books not in frequent use so as to reduce the movement of readers in them.

While the staff engaged on public service must have a reasonable amount of working space, this need not be very large, as the amount of clerical work they can do there is limited by the heavy demands of the public in a busy library. Most librarians prefer to separate service routine from general clerical work as much as possible; high standards of accuracy are needed in this type of library and it is not easy to achieve them if there are constant interruptions by readers needing attention. Moreover, assistants on public service, harassed by the thought of arrears of administrative duties which may have been allotted to them, are hardly likely to give adequate attention to readers' needs. If conditions permit, it is useful to have a small room or alcove behind the service counter where files of material in frequent use and staff indexes are at hand. Beside this should come the workroom for staff engaged in purely administrative duties, in which such noisy or untidy jobs as typing, repairs, and sorting and checking of periodical files can be done.

As the library grows it may not be possible to place all the stock on open shelves and storage room for books in reserve will be needed. It may be that there is ready access from the counter to the main book stack, either directly or by lift or book conveyor, in which case the only problem is to find ways of ensuring that the time taken to deliver a book to a reader is as short as possible; if there is no main stack, a small stack room beside the workroom will be most useful. In a busy library of this type much more staff shelving and store space are required than is usual in departmental libraries, because of the large part that periodical files play in the library's work, and the amount of space they occupy.

If there is no possibility of providing adequate working or storage room and the public room is large, part of it might be screened off and used for this purpose, but the partition should always be carried to the ceiling.

COMMERCIAL AND TECHNICAL LIBRARIES

Another desirable provision is one or more small, sound-proof rooms, in which a translator or abstractor can dictate to a stenographer, or typing can be done by library users. These rooms can also serve for interviews or as research rooms for readers using a large amount of material.

Frequent requests are received for photographic or micro-film copies of scientific and technical articles and other matter. It is presumed that a special department will have been organised and equipped to do this work in the central building. In planning a new library the need for such provision should not be overlooked.

Position in the building

The position of the commercial and technical library in the main library building is of great importance. It may be considered from two angles: (1) its accessibility to the public, and (2) its relation to other departments of the service.

It is an axiom of library planning that the most used departments should be on the ground floor and as near to the main entrance as possible. The extent to which this principle can be applied in a particular building partially depends on the relative use of other departments. For example, if there is a very busy central lending library, that department would obviously take positional priority, and as the commercial and technical department is usually in more constant use—particularly for quick reference enquiries and periodicals—than the general

PLAN AND FURNITURE

reference library, the latter can therefore be placed on an upper floor if the building is of more than one storey.

In the event of two separate departments being organised, the difference between the commercial and technical sides of the work will again affect the placing of the departments. If the commercial library shelves the directories (which in at least one library are placed in the main hall in order to take traffic away from a library room) there will be a heavy use of these and other quick reference books such as telegraphic codes, timetables, etc., and the library should therefore be as near the entrance hall as possible. The same considerations apply, though to a lesser degree, to the technical library, particularly during the latter days of the week when large numbers of readers will consult the periodicals, not only for scientific and technical study, but also to read advertisements and professional news items. On balance, however, it seems reasonable to give traffic priority to the commercial library. If the general building plan allows, both the departments should be on the ground floor. If the library is a joint one, the part of the commercial stock in greatest use should be shelved near the entrance, and the farther end of the room should form the technical library.

Book stack

It has already been pointed out that the stock of the technical library, which must contain runs of files of many periodicals, is likely to grow rapidly and that if the main stack is used for storage, easy access to it is necessary. The problem of the book stack, which has long dominated library planning, has been largely resolved by the American experiments in "modular" or "adaptive" planning of libraries. Indeed, so many practical ideas of value in the functioning of libraries can be incorporated in buildings of this type, that most of the factors formerly affecting planning are now either inapplicable or have been so greatly modified that a reappraisal of them is needed, and the librarian building a new library would be well advised to study in detail some of the new American libraries built in this style. It is possible, in an "adaptive" library, to place the book stack or part of it anywhere in the building, and to adjust the size or layout of a department at any time without considerable structural changes. Hence, many of the suggestions contained in this chapter, which are based on the assumption that a new library will be a "monumental" building, will not apply if the librarian or architect can convince the local authority that in planning a modern public library the effectiveness of its internal arrangements is as important as is the production layout of a factory. The overriding principle governing the relationship of the library departments to the stack is that the utmost economy of time and labour in providing service from the stack to the reader should be aimed at. In a normal type of building of several floors it may be possible to arrange for all the reference libraries to receive their stack services from one lift, thus reducing power and staff costs, and avoiding the expense of conveyors.

Staff workrooms

The relationship between the staff service and that of the other departments in the building is also worthy of attention. The more the general library plan allows the staffs of several departments to work in adjoining rooms, the easier it is to arrange for staff coverage during difficult service times without unduly disturbing the work of the departments concerned. When a departmental staff is entirely self-contained the problem of relief is a serious one; if the staffs of more than one department work side by side, as it were, there are fewer of the inter-departmental jealousies and little frictions which are so frequent a source of trouble in large libraries whenever relief switches of staff have to be made. In the technical library detailed enquiries involving a great deal of research are often received. If several difficult questions are asked in quick succession at a time when the staff is weakened by illness or holidays, it is most helpful if an assistant from another department can be called across without waste of time or unnecessary argument to deal with simpler requests at the counter.

There is another reason why it is useful to have the workrooms of several departments adjacent to one another. Frequent exchanges of books and consultations among the staff are needed to get the best use of the library's resources. Though mechanical aids such as house telephones, electric recorders and quick service staff lifts are helpful, they cannot be an effective substitute for the regular personal contacts among staffs working in close proximity. When a new central building is being planned, it is an excellent principle to have several staff workrooms at a central point, with the public rooms surrounding them.

Lighting

In a building devoted to the use of books, good natural and artificial lighting is a primary need. If the site is a reasonably open one, the architect should have no difficulty in providing adequate natural light to the main rooms; modern methods of building construction and new materials such as glass brick have simplified his task. It may be noted that in the "adaptive" library little or no account is taken of natural light; there are no light wells, as these would interfere with the principle of complete flexibility which is its essential feature.

The system of artificial lighting should be considered at a very early stage of building, as the lighting ducts and points must generally be placed in position before the concrete floors are run. It is rather surprising that the services of a lighting expert are rarely used, though it should be possible to install a scientifically perfect system of artificial lighting capable of giving the requisite standard of illumination throughout. The position of the

PLAN AND FURNITURE

lighting points and the types of fittings to be used are sometimes decided almost casually, and the efficiency of the latter is made secondary to the architect's aesthetic judgment. Specialist services such as those of the steel construction and heating and ventilating engineers are always employed in the erection of a great building and there appear to be equally strong arguments for bringing in an illuminating engineer as consultant at an early stage of the planning.

As changes of point positions cannot easily be made once they have been fixed in a modern building, reserve lighting points should be provided freely. This also applies to electric heating and power points. It is advisable, too, to be generous with switches, even to the extent of switching practically every point separately, but when this is done in a very large room some master switches should also be installed. If general lighting is adopted, care should be taken to ensure that points are coupled up for switching in relation to the natural lighting. The library may, for instance, be placed in a rectangular room with natural light on one side only; on a dull day, the half of the room furthest from the windows will need artificial light, while in the other half the natural light may be quite good. An architect usually groups lights for switching across the room, but it is better to couple them along its length so that the darker portion may be lighted artificially without current being wasted near the windows.

If table lights are used for close work, some general

lighting is needed as well. One objection to table lighting is that it limits changes in the arrangement of the furniture; another, frequently expressed, is that it induces eye-strain. Point lighting fixed on bookcases is not usually satisfactory, for it fails to give an even standard of light on all the shelves. In general lighting the height, position and type of the fittings must be carefully considered to prevent shadows being thrown on the shelves by readers consulting books there.

The design of the fittings must be in accordance with the architect's general scheme, but an efficient light output should be insisted on. It should not be impossible for experts to design electric light fittings which are decorative, efficient, economical and easy to clean. The last is important, as a film of dust reduces efficiency.

Many library lighting problems, particularly the difficulty of ensuring an even spread of light throughout, have been solved by the introduction of fluorescent lighting. Hot cathode tubes, however, have limited power, and the numbers required to obtain a suitable standard of lighting at reading level hardly add to the appearance of a room so equipped. If the height of the library allows, cold cathode fluorescent ceiling fixtures provide a highly efficient light, but the colour of the tubes must be carefully chosen under expert advice so that the right light quality is obtained for reading and harmonises with the scheme of decoration. In this case there is an entire absence of pendants. If the ceiling is high, cold cathode installations can be obtained in a variety of pleasing pendant forms. The relative costs of fluorescent as against tungsten lamp lighting should be compared in relation to installation cost, maintenance and current consumption. Fluorescent equipment, particularly cold cathode, is expensive, and some library committees find the cost prohibitive.

FURNITURE

Few of the fittings required in the commercial and technical library are special to it, but in view of modern trends in library furniture, some comments are offered on the general equipment of the room.

General shelving

Most librarians have warm preferences as to whether shelving should be of wood or metal, perpendicular or raked, adjustable or fixed. The choice is mainly a matter of personal taste or prejudice; provided that the books are easily accessible, the decisions on all three points are not of overwhelming importance. In any case, as the shelving is the major part of the furniture, the architect's views must generally be allowed to prevail unless his proposals would affect adversely the library's work.

Hardwood shelving can be made to conform to the architectural scheme more readily than metal, and there is no clash of material or colour between it and building fittings, such as doors and architraves, and the rest of the furniture. If an all metal library could be designed so as to give a proper feeling to the material, it might be aesthetically satisfying, but it is hard to resist a sense of incongruity when shelves are of steel and the tables and other furniture are of wood. It is not easy, and is expensive, to make changes in steel shelving should these become necessary, or to fix special features such as display fittings in it. When alterations are made the colour cannot always be exactly matched; moreover, the colour chosen conditions the decoration of the library in the future. The light neutral shades which some manufacturers offer soon become soiled where the books rub the shelf surfaces. Wooden shelving, on the other hand, can be altered without difficulty and the new portions matched perfectly with the existing shelving.

Should the shelving be perpendicular or raked? The size of the room affects the decision on this matter, for if it is small, six or even seven shelves per tier may be needed to accommodate the open shelf stock. The minimum rake should be one inch per shelf, and the loss of six or seven inches around all the shelving would reduce the floor area considerably, particularly if double-sided cases are used. The ideal type of raked shelving is a tier of five shelves, with the lowest 1' 6" from the floor; the reader can see and handle all books on it with comfort.

Adjustable shelving has been standard for so long that librarians almost automatically insist on it in new buildings. In practice, the shelves are seldom adjusted, even in the stack, because of the labour involved in doing so. Adjustable shelves save much space in a "fixed location" library where the height of a shelf, once filled with books, rarely needs changing, but frequent adjustments of one or more shelves must be made when larger books are added to the classified sequence of a large library with a rapidly growing stock. The same consideration applies to the open shelves, and there are two further disadvantages: the degree of adjustability in tiers of five shelves is limited and if there are varied shelf levels in different tiers, the library looks very untidy. Some librarians, who believe that movable shelves serve no useful purpose under modern conditions, have reverted to fixed shelving, which is cheaper to make. The few outsize books can be accommodated separately in a number of tiers with deeper adjustable shelves.

Directory shelving

Because of the constant use made of them, it is usual to shelve directories and other quick reference business books such as telegraphic codes, time tables, telephone directories and certain annuals, in a special fitting near the entrance. Several persons may be consulting the directories at the same time, and it is therefore advisable to spread the shelving laterally, and as most of the books are large and heavy, two shelves, the lower one a little above reading height when standing, are recommended, though, if space permits, one shelf is better. The normal kind of enquiry—searching for an address—takes so little time to answer that many users do not trouble to carry the directory to a table; hence a combined directory shelf or shelves and reading slope may be found useful. The bottom shelf must be raised above the top edge of the reading slope to the width of the thickest book likely to be shelved, so that if a volume is left on the slope—as frequently happens—it will not be in the way of a reader who wishes to take another book from the shelf immediately behind it. In libraries where the directories and other business quick reference books are not so heavily used, or where there is not enough space for long runs of shelving, three or perhaps four shelves might be provided behind a flat or gently sloping reading space at which the reader can sit when using the books. Here, again, it is advisable to lift the bottom shelf at least four inches above the table top. Other libraries merely provide normal shelving and readers use the books on adjacent tables.

Display fittings

Special fittings for occasional displays of books, illustrations or other matter are useful, particularly in the commercial library, in which certain books, such as those on advertising or with isotype statistics, lend themselves to this purpose. Similar displays of important material are sometimes desirable in the technical library. The fittings may either be in the form of fixtures in a tier of the wall shelv-

PLAN AND FURNITURE

ing, or movable, double-sided stands which can be placed anywhere in the room. The first type may consist of large panels for posters with shelves below them. They do not interfere with the oversight of the room, and make a welcome break in the plain run of wall shelves. In one design the panel of cork linoleum is recessed to the back of the shelving; there are two shelves below, one in the form of a slope with a narrow ledge at the bottom on which books can be shown open, and the other an ordinary shelf which, if slightly tilted, can be used either for books shelved in the normal way or open.

If adjustable shelving is used, and the tiers are of uniform width, it is a good plan to make a lightly constructed fitting of this type as a separate unit which can be placed in any tier of the wall shelving after removing some of the shelves. Being movable, it can be related to any section of the stock; if more shelving space is needed, the fitting can be taken away for a time and the tier used for its proper purpose. It is common knowledge that permanent fixtures soon cease to be noticed, and there is much to be said for the flexibility and freshness this idea gives. In fixed shelving (or even in adjustable shelving) an even simpler form of movable display can be made of a cork lino panel with side supports, which will slip into a shelf and fill the whole of the space, the panel being flush with the front edges. Posters can be fixed on it, and the shelf below used for the material on show. Cork linoleum is a suitable medium for poster panels, as drawing pins or other fasteners do not readily mark its surface, and it can easily be replaced or painted. Many kinds of island display fittings have been designed for libraries and there is no lack of examples to choose from. It is advisable to make them low in order to allow oversight, but this limits the size of the poster panel. They thus lack some of the attractiveness which the large poster panel gives to the wall fittings, which can be made to the full height of the shelving.

Even in a special library, many readers remain unaware of the range of information available outside their own fields of study and it is sometimes useful to show certain important publications in odd corners of the room when the design of the shelving allows. Occasional book slopes may be fixed on return walls or panels; they can be used for books in constant use, such as atlases. The ends of projecting bookcases, or wide panels among the wall shelving, which may mask ventilation or other ducts, sometimes give an opportunity for one or more occasional shelves, with a display panel above. Generally, a shelf is preferable to a slope, since a slope can never be used for the normal purposes of a shelf, whereas a shelf can always be used to display books open by placing a movable slope or book rest on it or by constructing it with a slight backward tilt. Librarians, who have lost none of the mechanical ingenuity which gave us the indicator, have devised many ways of using a variety of movable display fittings for individual items and it is useful to have an adequate supply of them.

A tier reserved for recent additions is always useful. It can be made noticeable by its design: it may project from, or be recessed into, the wall shelving, or differ from it in width of tier, or carry above it a projecting cornice with concealed strip lighting which illuminates the books and immediately attracts the eye. Some libraries show books in floodlit glass cases at suitable points. These are usually built into a wall but in this kind of library books should be available for handling, and the glass front is perhaps better omitted. Many excellent examples of illuminated cases and floodlit displays can be seen in modern stores where the librarian furnishing a new library can find plenty of useful ideas.

Tables and chairs

Some librarians may prefer to use large flat or sloping tables seating several readers, with or without divisions along their length; others may incline towards separate tables, or double tables for two readers facing each other with a partition between them.

There seems to be no conclusive evidence of readers' preferences for individual as against general tables, or vice versa. The former are uneconomical of space and as they cannot be large they are not helpful to the reader consulting many books at one time; a small shelf must be provided in them for books awaiting use. Large flat open tables seating six or more readers give plenty of space for books and other material, provided that not all the seats are occupied at one time. Table lighting by the trough method, which houses concealed strip lighting, helps to avoid the embarrassment frequently felt by readers who work facing one another. It may be thought desirable to provide a mixture of tables so that readers may have a choice: a number of individual tables for those engaged on intense study, and flat double-sided tables for users of directories and periodicals. The shape and size of the room affects the choice of table to some extent, but whatever type is chosen, a reasonable amount of room should be allowed to each reader. The minimum space should be 2′ 3″ × 1′ 9″. At least one large table should be provided where readers can consult loose maps or plans and make tracings from them if this is permitted.

Many readers will work in a commercial and technical library for long periods at a time. It is reasonable, therefore, to give them the comfort of chairs designed to give ease to the body when in a sitting position, and equipped with padded or sprung seats. Physical comfort and hard thinking are not necessarily incompatible. Simplicity in design is aesthetically satisfying, and makes the chair easier to clean.

Periodical racks

As periodicals are an important part of the stock, and their number is large compared with those in

PLAN AND FURNITURE

the other departments, their adequate display raises a number of difficult problems. The normal method of spreading them on the surfaces of reading tables, or placing them upright against a central rail or in a cavity in the table centre, is unsuitable in the special library, where tables are needed for other purposes as well.

If new special fittings cannot be obtained and the librarian is compelled to use makeshift methods, one simple and cheap way is to put the periodicals on ordinary shelves in cloth covered boxes, each holding several titles. If sufficient shelf space is available to allow one box for each title some back numbers can be placed alongside the current one. Other alternatives involve the use of covers or cases, usually in quarter leather with cloth boards, into which the copy can be slipped. The cases can be shelved like books, but either the tiers must be very narrow or supports should be fixed at intervals on the shelves to keep the cases upright.

Cased periodicals can also be displayed in the old-fashioned but effective fitting known as a "toast-rack"—a long narrow table, with metal or wooden upright divisions—the cases, lettered on the spine, being placed on their fore-edges. Another simple rack is in the form of a long wooden box along the length of a table, containing a number of narrow tiered compartments each of which holds a periodical standing upright. If preferred, the front of the fitting can be slightly raked. A more recent and attractive rack consists of a series of curved oak uprights 2' 3" high, with ten flat glass shelves, spaced 1½" apart, slotted between them. Each tier holds eleven periodicals, the titles being shown on ivorine labels affixed to the front edges of the glass shelves.[1]

The ideal fitting would, of course, allow the reader to identify the publication he wants without trouble and give him access to some of the immediate back numbers. Such a method, in use in an American library, consists of a series of wooden wall slopes one above the other allowing the whole of the largest periodical to be seen. The slopes are divided into sections to hold two magazines and are hinged at the top. When a reader lifts a slope, he finds back numbers on a shelf behind, and thus has ready access to a considerable range of periodical literature without calling on the staff service. A later development of this idea, in which the slopes are divided into tiers wide enough to hold three periodicals, is now in use.[2] In this case the slopes are pivoted on the uprights and remain open when lifted to a certain level. This system is excellent, but it takes up so much room that it is very doubtful whether it is practicable except in libraries with plenty of space or few magazines.

Another arrangement, which has been in use in a busy special library for many years, is reasonably compact and seems to meet all the librarian's diffi-

[1] This table periodical rack is described and illustrated in the *Library Association Record*, 1953, p. 397.
[2] *Library Journal*, Vol. 77, 1952, p. 2097.

PLAN AND FURNITURE

culties, consists of a series of ledges with slopes behind with sufficient backward rake on them to prevent the magazines from falling forward over the metal guards which hold them in place. Glass can be used instead of metal strips across the lower part of the slopes; it allows the cover to be seen equally well, but the task of frequently cleaning such a quantity of glass is no light one. The amount of overlap of the periodicals when they are standing on the slopes has been carefully calculated on the basis of the largest one in use and all the titles and a fair amount of the cover are clearly visible. The slopes are in tiers 3′ 7″ wide, each with a capacity of 24 periodicals; the slopes are 9″ in height. The rake projection of this six tier rack is 1′ 6″, and the lowest slope is 1′ 2″ from the floor. The ledges are 1″ wide, but some periodicals are now so thick—the American *Electronics* and *Iron Age* and the British *Journal of the Chemical Society*, for example—that it is difficult to fit them into the space between the slope and the metal strips without damaging the cover and front pages. The ledges should therefore be made 1½″ wide; this will increase the projection of a six slope rack to 1′ 9″.

In this fitting the periodicals are arranged in alphabetical order, and to help readers to replace used ones, metal holders bearing their titles are slipped over the metal supporting strips, which have square edges for this purpose. This allows complete flexibility, which is important in view of the frequent changes in the titles taken.

Directory shelves with reading slope—Science and Commerce Library, Sheffield. See p. 87

COMMERCIAL AND TECHNICAL LIBRARIES

In making his choice of the best kind of periodical rack for his purpose, the librarian should have in mind the following points. A system which makes periodical covers necessary has two weaknesses. Good cases are costly, and as they must be lettered, the reader is not helped in identifying the magazine he wants if he has to find it among several hundred more all lettered in the same way. The advantage of the open type of rack, in which all the periodicals are clearly seen, is that the one required can be instantly recognised because each has a familiar distinctive cover. Cases are not really needed for the weeklies which replace themselves before their covers become soiled or torn. Some librarians paste a copy of the cover of the periodical on the face of the case and varnish it, but it soon looks unsightly. The new clear plastic cases are useful, but they are expensive and the plastic loses its clarity through use.

Map fittings

Most commercial libraries stock many maps of various sizes. Some of them are too large to be used flat on a table. The most satisfactory way of dealing with large maps is to mount them on rollers so that they can be stored away without damage, and to provide a high fitting into which the top roller can be slotted. The map hangs down and is easily consulted. The holding mechanism should be made adjustable to take maps of different widths; the rolled maps can be stored in a long cupboard at the

Sheffield Science and Commerce Library—training students from the College of Commerce in the use of business books.

PLAN AND FURNITURE

base of the fitting. A simpler method is to provide ordinary hooks on a wall to hold the top roller. If certain maps are constantly in use, it is helpful to have a similar frame to hold the spring rollers to which they are attached. Each map can be identified by a label suspended on a cord by means of which the reader can draw it down.

In one library, roller maps are kept in a series of large drawers, provided with adjustable clips at the sides into which the rollers are slotted. An index to the maps so stored is fixed behind glass on the top of the large fitting holding the drawers. This is of table height and the maps are consulted on it. It is also used for smaller maps stored under different conditions near by.

Smaller maps and plans can be filed in one of the many standard type map and plan files on the market. The vertical plan file has a large capacity and the maps or plans in it can be readily consulted without the necessity of handling others, which is the main objection to storing them in flat drawer files. Smaller filing cabinets, containing two drawers each 20" × 25" are also available. They, like the larger vertical files, have stout manilla folders to hold the maps. These are supported by numbers of double manilla guides with strong springs inside them. The constant pressure of the springs keeps the maps flat, but care is needed when replacing them to avoid folding or creasing. The choice must depend on needs and personal preferences, as there are advantages and disadvantages in both the vertical and flat methods of filing. Some librarians are reverting to the "old fashioned" method of storing plans flat. When drawers are used for this purpose, it is not easy to withdraw a particular map, and even more difficult to replace it, without creasing it or others, unless all the maps are taken out. The older method was to make holders consisting of two large cloth covered boards hinged together like a large book cover. The bottom board is provided with cloth flaps on the open sides. These are folded over the maps which are placed on the bottom board, and when the top board is lowered, the two are tied together with tapes on the three open sides. They are then stored on flat map shelves large enough to take them. Provided that the number of maps placed in each holder is limited, the cases are easy to handle and the maps in them are rarely damaged.

Catalogue

It is not proposed to deal with details of standard fittings, such as card or sheaf catalogue cases, which have been described and discussed in detail in many text-books. It may be thought advisable to design a stand which will hold the catalogue and provide shelving for the bibliographies, abstracts and periodical and other indexes which will be stocked, particularly in the technical library.

Staff service point

The methods of administration adopted will govern the position and design of the staff counter

PLAN AND FURNITURE

or enclosure. If the American practice of using the library jointly for reference and home study is adopted, an island enclosure on the lines of those in use in lending libraries may be necessary, and there is no lack of excellent examples in modern libraries to choose from. Provision would, of course, have to be made in it for card or slip indexes. It may not be thought advisable to isolate the public service staff, particularly in a library with a wide range of external contacts; it creates many problems, and there are strong arguments for placing the service point in a position which gives direct contact with the filing, stack and work rooms. In this case, there is no need to house the staff indexes in the counter itself and it can be fitted quite simply with cupboards and shelves to hold material needed for routine jobs. Open shelves in so prominent a part of the furniture soon become untidy, and those who believe that neatness is next to godliness in librarianship are advised to cover them with hinged wooden flaps fitted with spring catches. There should, of course, be at least two desk spaces, preferably in wells a few inches lower than the counter top, where the service assistants can perform their limited clerical duties without covering the counter with their records. The service point should be indicated by a clear and well designed sign with some such word as "service", "enquiries", or "information", for it is unfortunately true that despite a century of public library service, only a comparatively small percentage of people realise that books

COMMERCIAL AND TECHNICAL LIBRARIES

are sources of information of all kinds and that the library is the proper place to come to for it.

The design of other fittings must depend on the requirements of the service the librarian develops, and his own observation and ingenuity.

CHAPTER IV

STAFF

THE selection of staff with the requisite qualities and training is so important to the success of the work of the commercial and technical library that it is dealt with in some detail in relation to the needs of the department. Though the duties of the librarian of the general reference and of the special library are in many ways similar, the differences are sufficiently notable to justify careful examination.

The nature of the service

In a general reference library, in which almost the whole range of knowledge is covered by the book stock, the librarian is expected to have a high standard of judgment of book values in all the subjects represented. He must be able to produce the material needed by those undertaking study and research, to assist the reader to select it, and to provide answers, or books that may give the answers, to a wide variety of questions asked by non-student—and often quite casual—users of the department.

The librarian of the commercial and technical library deals with a comparatively limited range of subjects, but the number of books in each of them is generally much greater than in the reference library; in addition, he has to be familiar with, and select from, a range of specialised material in the form of periodicals and the publications of governments, societies, chambers of commerce, research associations and the like. Hence, he should possess a more detailed knowledge of the subjects included in his library and the literature about them than the reference librarian.

The commercial and technical librarian, too, is more frequently called upon to find specific information for his readers, and must use the books himself, and interpret their contents, in order to do so. To help in this work, he finds it advisable to compile detailed catalogues and indexes, and, if his service reaches so high a standard that it attracts industrial research workers, summaries or abstracts of material likely to be useful to them. In addition to the normal skills of librarianship, considerable factual or technical knowledge is needed to keep these records current; and this is essential if they are to be really useful.

So far as the above activities are concerned, the work of the commercial library and the technical library varies merely in degree, according to the use to which the services are put; and the training, experience and aptitudes of the staff which help to make the one efficient are usually equally valuable in the other. There is, however, one important difference between the two types of library. The majority of the users of a commercial library are

STAFF

not students, and are unfamiliar with the use of books; they ask for information on matters of fact readily gathered from well-known sources easily interpreted by a competent librarian. The number of enquiries entailing considerable research is small compared with the general volume of work done, and even when research is needed, the available sources of information are often comparatively easy to use.

For example, in the fields of applied economics, trade conditions in various countries, statistics, etc., the publications of certain government departments cover much of the ground, and record facts in a clear and handy way. It is unfortunate that in some subjects, notably in marketing research, the literature available for public use is often very limited and the gaps in the information it provides wide and disturbing, though firms engaged in competitive trading can obtain much of it through commercial agencies specialising in such work. A somewhat paradoxical situation thus arises: while, taken as a whole, the commercial enquiries received are simpler than those met with in the technical library, the percentage of failure in answering them is higher.

In the technical library, only a small part of the librarian's work is concerned with answering the fairly simple kind of question asked by what may be called the casual user. By far the greater proportion of readers are technicians and technical students who know their subjects, are mostly acquainted with the literature on them, and are therefore able to find the books and other material they require without difficulty. In addition to these two classes of library users, there is a small body of research workers, concerned with work in a limited field, who need the staff's help in tracing sources of specialised publications, and smaller firms without research facilities also come for information of a highly technical nature. Many of the enquiries they make can only be satisfied after patient and knowledgeable search. In this respect the technical librarian's work is closely akin to that of his reference library colleague, though in a narrower and more intensive field.

As many of the services given to users of both the commercial and the technical library are of a like kind, the same staff can administer a joint department quite effectively; in some ways there is considerable overlapping between the two branches. In cities where the number of readers justifies the provision of separate libraries, a larger proportion of them are likely to require more specialised information, and a correspondingly greater degree of specialisation in knowledge and training will be required of the staffs.

The factors governing the selection of the staff for the commercial and technical library may be summarised as follows:—

1. More precise knowledge of the literature of the subjects included is needed than in a general reference library.

STAFF

2. Detailed indexes, analytical catalogues and summaries must be compiled and kept current.

3. The staff must have the qualities required for quick reference work in the commercial library.

4. They must be competent to provide detailed information from their records and interpret it to the reader in both sections of the library.

5. They must have sufficient technical knowledge to trace specialised sources of information for the research worker, to advise the technician and the technical student in the selection and use of technical literature, and to obtain precise information of an advanced scientific and technical kind for industrial users.

Staff requirements—library technique

Consideration of the needs of the service suggests that the librarian must first of all have a thorough training in librarianship; but some aspects of that training require further analysis. Though technical competence in classification, cataloguing and indexing is of the highest importance, it should not be of the kind that all too frequently implies unimaginative orthodoxy. The type of indexing and analytical cataloguing required can rarely be done under the rules laid down for general library cataloguing. The effectiveness of such records for their purpose largely depends on alert anticipation of possible demands, and a quick mind and eye for the occasional useful items which are sometimes found in the most unlikely places. It would be undesirable to attempt to make analytical catalogue entries for every chapter, or part of a chapter, of all the books in the collection; yet unless each new book is examined to see whether it contains matter which strengthens sections of the library in which the literature is scanty, particularly in regard to local commerce or industry, and such material is intelligently selected and recorded in the catalogue, it is unlikely that the best value will be obtained from the library. The librarian must, if necessary, make his own rules, and use his trained intelligence to build up his catalogue into a real guide to the contents of the books, as well as to their title pages. To do this he must exercise a judgment rarely asked of the orthodox cataloguer since the mental discipline needed in the compilation of a dictionary catalogue was removed from the duties and training of British librarians.

When applying the classification (except in those libraries which use an advanced scheme such as the Universal Decimal Classification), the librarian is frequently compelled to sub-divide classes which have become overloaded because of the specialisation of his stock. The classification schemes in common use have sectional weaknesses which are comparatively unimportant in a general library, but they may

STAFF

handicap readers in a library where more precise definition of certain classes is sometimes needed. Rigidity in the interpretation of a normal library classification scheme should be avoided. The techniques of classification and cataloguing are not ends in themselves, but means to the end of making the books in the library serve to inform readers; they merely attempt to codify principles which experience has shown are generally applicable to the proper interpretation of a library's contents. When they fail to do this, as sometimes happens when readers' needs are specialised, the librarian should not hesitate to substitute his own methods for those of the theorists.

The skills employed in selecting matter for analytical entries, and in choosing suitable subject headings, are the same as those needed in the compilation of all kinds of information indexes; only the form of the entries is affected by the decision to place them either in the public catalogue or in a unified staff index of information. All special libraries need extensive indexes in one form or another; their extent, and their type, depend on how the library service develops, but their value is measured by the knowledge, intelligence and judgment the librarian brings to their compilation and use.

Other general library techniques are of course needed, but in the main they differ only in detail from those in common use. All the staff should have had experience in other departments and be fully aware of their scope.

COMMERCIAL AND TECHNICAL LIBRARIES

Personal qualities

In all reference libraries, in which a great deal of personal service is given, the librarian should be able to deal with the reader in a way that invites his confidence. This is particularly important in the commercial and technical library, where it is so large a part of the work. All librarians are familiar with the exasperating person who states his problem so obliquely that the real nature of the enquiry only emerges after much searching has been done, when it is usually found that it could have been answered in a few moments had it been clearly stated in the first place. In the technical, and to a lesser degree in the commercial library, this common difficulty is met with oftener than in a general reference library. One reason for it is that representatives of business houses, research workers and inventors sometimes wish to cover up the real nature of their enquiries in order to keep it from the knowledge of competitors, and they naturally look upon the librarian as a possible source of leakage of information. Assistants who have the rare gift of being able to encourage the enquirer to "open up" not only save a great deal of time, but are also able to deal more effectively with the enquiry because, unless its precise nature is made known, the information gathered can rarely be really useful.

In a library devoted to the needs of those engaged in business and industry, the way in which an enquiry is dealt with is by no means unimportant. Alertness and a pleasant and brisk manner are helpful.

STAFF

The mere fact that business men are impressed by speed and efficiency is worth attention; and neither can be acquired by any form of external education or text-book instruction.

Mental qualities and aptitudes

The "flair for finding" is perhaps the most important attribute of the commercial and technical librarian and his staff. Though it can be developed by training and experience, it is largely innate, and assistants who are not naturally endowed with it should be transferred to departments where other gifts are perhaps more useful. A librarian of a great city has said that in his view, for good service in a special library, "memory and observation are important, also a degree of imagination and intuitive insight". The word "intuition" has a somewhat unfortunate association in these days, but it well describes an aptitude of the utmost value. So important is it, and so rarely is it found, that the larger libraries often try out many assistants in the reference departments before discovering one who has this quality. It is closely allied to the questing intelligence of the scholar, but in this case it must be accompanied by a right sense of practical needs. This intuition or flair allows the assistant to follow an enquiry through to the end, to use his developed visual sense and memory to work on it in the most unlikely sources, and to worry over it mentally until a solution has been found. The good searcher is one with a quick, inquisitive mind, and a high sense of library book values. Important though all these attributes are, however, they are by no means the only things needed in dealing with personal enquiries and compiling adequate indexes and other essential records. It would be a mistake to assume that those who have them, but little else besides, will make good assistants in the commercial and technical library; but without these gifts they are unlikely ever to be good.

Background knowledge

It is generally and rightly accepted that a librarian must be "educated" in the sense of having a well-stored and critical mind, and those who work in a special library should not be less well endowed in this respect than their colleagues in other departments. Indeed, as their work is concerned with exploiting a limited field of knowledge for the benefit of many who are themselves experts, it is reasonable to expect that they should have a deeper and more detailed grasp of it than is usually possible in a general library. It is argued, with some degree of truth, that the general librarian can sometimes be handicapped by having exceptional knowledge of certain subjects, as it tends to give bias to his book selection. This argument does not apply to the special library, in which inclusiveness, rather than balance, is needed in portions of the stock.

There are divergent views as to what constitutes an "educated" librarian, some arguing that the term can only be properly applied to university graduates, and others that graduation cannot provide a real test of the possession either of the kind of knowledge or the type of mind needed for librarianship. Such discussions are largely sterile, because neither side appears to be capable of making a dispassionate judgment of the case on its merits.[1] It is not proposed to air these ancient and unprofitable prejudices again, but rather to attempt a brief examination of the qualities required of the worker in the commercial and technical library.

It surely does not matter whether the librarian acquires knowledge through reading alone or reading with the help of a teacher or lecturer, so long as he becomes a knowledgeable person. Rather absurdly, librarians sometimes claim, on the one hand, that a well-stocked library provides the best means of self-education, and on the other, that one can only educate oneself by attending lectures and undertaking courses of formal study of subjects that often appear to have little relevance to reasonable needs in the world to-day or to the mental growth of the student. The intelligent librarian who reads widely and critically, and gives some time to reflection, is likely to discover a form of mental self-reliance of the utmost value in his work. But many well-read people do not properly apply the knowledge they absorb; they merely fill their minds with facts which remain mental lumber unless they can be

[1] The reader interested in this matter is advised to read Mary Walton's temperate article "This graduate problem" in the *Library Association Record*, 1934, pp. 166–169.

co-ordinated into a coherent and well-reasoned line of thought. Similarly, those who have continued their studies at a university for an additional three years are not necessarily better informed because of it unless they have allowed their reading to stray wider than the courses set. Even then there can be no guarantee that they have formed any kind of critical judgment, or have developed good mental habits. Observation of the work of the products of these different methods of self-education—for all education is self-inflicted—may lead to the conclusion that the one is no more capable of producing persons with wide knowledge and good minds than the other. The wise librarian will not appoint his staff on the basis of any certified test of the possession of a certain amount of knowledge, professional or other—though minimum requirements must be satisfied—but by whether or not they have intelligent and enquiring minds, developed by critical reading, and are capable of thinking outside the range of conventional acceptances.

In the commercial library, where much of the work is of a quick reference type, background knowledge of commercial subjects, though desirable if the other qualities are there, should not be the prior consideration. The library may be more efficient if the librarian is a good librarian first, and a good student afterwards. As he will have an alert and receptive mind, he will soon be able to acquire sufficient knowledge of the contents of the comparatively limited range of books in his library

STAFF

to provide the needful background to his service.

These considerations also apply to some extent to the type of technical library which confines its work to the technician and technical student; but in those which attract research workers and industrialists, the librarian may find himself at a loss when dealing with them unless he has had some scientific training.

In a technical library much used by specialists it is sometimes hard for a layman to interpret many of the ideas and discoveries its material contains unless he has found sufficient interest in them to undertake courses of study. The needs of research in a library concerned with humane studies rarely demand specialised knowledge on the part of the librarian; bibliographical competence and judgment are certainly required, but they can be acquired by persons with the right type of mind and education while working in the library. But a background of scientific training is often useful to the librarian of a research technical library, just as historical training is needed in an archivist. It is true that the great advances in scientific knowledge and its practical applications have narrowed research to an extent that makes it difficult for a worker in one field to judge the value of work done, and the literature about it, in another. Nevertheless, this does not invalidate the point of view here advanced that a general scientific training will help the librarian to select and use his book stock, and assist his readers, more effectively than he could do without it. There are, of course, exceptions to this statement, since the human mind is so unpredictable that it is unsafe to generalise.

Practice in this country offers little guidance. Only two libraries employ assistants with science degrees in their commercial and technical libraries. So many factors have to be taken into account in the selection of staff that it seems inadvisable to attempt to lay down any hard and fast rules. The decision as to whom to employ should be based on the needs of the service, and on a careful assessment of the abilities—in so far as they are capable of test —of candidates to deal with them. In a library in a district with a single dominant industry, which would be reflected in the book stock and the use of the library, the range of research would be correspondingly narrow, and there would appear to be advantages in having at its head a person who had done some work in the subject, provided that he was not lacking in other essential ways. It is usual, in such a library, to enlist the aid of specialists when selecting and discarding books and a librarian with a scientific training would be better able to check the value of such advice (for experts, being human, are liable to error and prejudice like others) and moreover could meet the majority of his readers on an advanced common ground. Where a library caters for such a variety of industries that a high degree of specialisation is unlikely to be reached, the need for scientific training is much less obvious, as the work is likely to be of a general reference library character within the range of technical subjects covered.

A library organisation demands, above all things, high standards of accuracy in its working, and this is a matter of good habit acquired by long training in a well-administered library. Hence, whatever conclusion is reached about the relative importance of scientific training and library practice, the qualities that can be developed by experience should never be discounted. It would certainly be an unmistakable sign of zeal in a librarian trained on normal lines if he voluntarily undertook a course of study in science or technology. The parallel interest of a graduate in the essentials of librarianship, or his lack of it, can unfortunately only be proved after his appointment, which partly explains the hesitation some librarians feel in accepting graduates without other evidence of their aptitudes.

Men or women librarians

In this country, most commercial and technical libraries are staffed by men. The argument most frequently used in support of male staffs is that the majority of the readers are men and prefer to be served by male assistants. This prejudice does not exist in America, but it is still in evidence in Britain, though of late years it has become less strong. It used to be commonly believed that women have no aptitude for scientific matters, but the number now receiving higher education in science shows that this belief is unfounded. One practical point of

COMMERCIAL AND TECHNICAL LIBRARIES

importance is that however efficient the indexes, catalogues, abstracts and other records, they can be made much more fruitful if they are supplemented by the librarian's memory and observation. As it takes time and much practice among the books to build up a mental guide to the library's contents, continuity of staff service is desirable. The heavy loss of competent women staff through marriage seriously affects the efficiency of a library which depends so much on the specialised knowledge they acquire, and men are sometimes preferred to women for this reason alone.

Theoretical training

Professional qualifications in librarianship are awarded by the Library Association and by the School of Librarianship and Archives, University College, London. Those of the former may be obtained either through private study, or through full-time attendance at one of the Library Schools. Correspondence classes conducted by the Association of Assistant Librarians and part-time classes arranged at various colleges throughout the country are available for the student undertaking private study. Entrance to the London University School of Librarianship is open to honours graduates. A qualifying period of one year in an approved library and five passes in the General Certificate of Education (except for graduates) are required of students who wish to sit for the Library Association examinations.

STAFF

The Library Association examinations syllabus has now been broadened to include sections suitable for those who wish to specialise in the work of commercial and technical libraries. The Registration Examination (Group D) provides a test in the literature of science. In Part 2 of the Final examination there is a paper on special libraries and information bureaux, and in Part 3 the student may sit either for literature and librarianship of the social sciences, including commerce and law (useful in the commercial library), or literature and librarianship of science and technology. It will be seen that in order to qualify for work in a commercial and technical library through these examinations, the assistant must progress beyond the Registration Examination.

The syllabus of the School of Librarianship of University College, London, has also recently been revised, and training for special librarianship is now given equal place with other subjects. Previously, one paper offered an alternative between (a) public library administration, and (b) university and special library administration. The second section has now been divided, and the "special" libraries course extends over three terms instead of one. Apart from this option, all students cover the same courses of study.

The London School of Librarianship instruction in special libraries does not lay any emphasis on the work of commercial and technical departments in public libraries. It is a more general course designed to cover the main principles of special library techniques, and, in general, one descriptive lecture only is devoted to a particular type of library.

The Association of Special Libraries and Information Bureaux provides training courses which last a week, twice a year. The Association has recently given consideration to the establishment of a system of examination for information officers. It is argued, with some degree of truth, that the kind of library training provided by the Library Association and the London University School of Librarianship examinations is not wholly, and in some cases not even partially, relevant to the work of an information officer, and that examinations based on an entirely different syllabus are needed. Though this divergence of views does not really concern those intending to qualify for service in a commercial and technical library, for which, as has already been suggested, a good basic training in librarianship is essential, it is mentioned here because some technical librarians, trained in public libraries, may wish to apply for similar posts in industry. It may perhaps also be useful if the distinction between a special librarian and an information officer is made plain.

The provision of libraries for the research and technical staffs in industry has increased rapidly during recent years. Some industrialists find it hard to realise that the tools of research, in the form of an adequate library and a competent, trained librarian, are needed by firms which wish to survive in an age of scientific and technical development.

STAFF

It is not uncommon for persons to be appointed as "librarian" or "information officer" who have no training or qualifications in librarianship. In all but the largest firms, some of which have splendid libraries, the range of material in works libraries is generally not large, and the duties of the information officer are mainly devoted to finding sources of material and making abstracts from journals, and circularising the results to the various departments. The abilities needed for this work are not necessarily those required by a special librarian, who, in addition to acting as an information officer, must organise and control a library, sometimes of considerable size. If a clear definition of the kind of work to be done by persons using the description "information officer", as distinct from "librarian", could be made and generally accepted, the creation of an examination system for information officers would be a wise step. It is difficult, however, to make such a definition; and the rather limited syllabus which would probably be suitable for information officers would not be likely to provide an adequate test of the training and competence of the librarians of some of the major libraries of scientific institutions, research associations and industrial extablishments. Some sensible comments on this matter appear in paragraphs 50–53 of the Report by the Panel on Technical Information Services of the Committee on Industrial Productivity.[1] It is to be hoped, however, that all concerned will reach agreement

[1] *Journal of documentation*, Vol. 7, 1951, pp. 109–110.

on systems of training and examination appropriate to the needs of both types of workers in their respective spheres; it is not enough to try to base a distinction on the word "documentation".[1] So far as anyone has attempted to define it, it appears to mean the exercise of a minor part of the duties librarians have been doing for years.

Practical training

The value of written examinations has been called into question by persons of eminence in education, whose opinions naturally merit consideration. The element of luck in the questions set, the ease with which those who have photographic minds can absorb facts, the advantage the skilled writer has over the pen-tied, can all be used as arguments against the system. A written test too often merely assesses the candidate's ability to pass an examination —that is, his possession of the skills which go to that task. These skills, and the study the student must undertake, have value. Knowledge and intellectual awareness are needed in all branches of library work, and the examination system does at least weed out those without them; moreover, no one has been able to discover a more effective method of assessing

---

[1] The first part of Professor Edy Velander's address on "The Information Service and the Contact Organisation of the Royal Swedish Academy of Engineering Sciences, Stockholm" (International symposium on the organisation of scientific and industrial research, O.E.E.C.) gives some idea of the way in which "documentation" is used to describe techniques which seem to vary little from normal library practice.

STAFF

certain abilities, however limited the test may be. So the examination system must stay, intelligently planned, one hopes, in relation to the needs of the profession. The syllabuses for examinations in librarianship are based on the accepted methods of academic institutions, and take little account of other aptitudes needed, some of which cannot be measured by any written test. A really adequate system of professional education would therefore include actual detailed work and training in libraries selected for the competence of their administration, where good habits of mind and action could be encouraged, and the student could learn to exercise administrative judgment and acquire a proper sense of values in the practical problems which he would have to solve in the course of his normal duties.

The successful practice of librarianship requires qualities not commonly found together in one person; good intellectual equipment and practical ability. An entrant who is endowed with a naturally good mind and is eager to learn should, in all but a very few exceptional cases, become a competent librarian if properly trained. It is unfortunate that many people with a literary or general bookish bent assume that this is all that is needed in librarianship —a misapprehension unfortunately shared by some appointments officers. The fact is, of course, that practical aptitudes are absolutely essential for a large part of the librarian's work, though they perhaps take a larger place in the administrative departments or the home reading and other general service libraries than in the special library.

Whatever his previous literary or bookish background, the assistant can only obtain what may be called "a library sense of book values" by working in a library and by constantly exercising his mind in learning to recognise the distinction between his own preferences in books and their value for library purposes. In the special library, one with wide intellectual interests is preferable to another whose reading has been almost exclusively devoted to pure literature. He should be encouraged to study the stock and appraise the value of individual books, apart from what he learns about them in the course of his duties, in order to gain a discriminating knowledge of the library's contents. Though there may be a place, even in the commercial and technical library, for a few purely routine assistants, with little book knowledge and no ambition to have any, who can do the background administrative work well and deal with simple enquiries, it is better to select those who express a preference for the work and have the requisite abilities, as the number of staff can never be large enough to carry any assistants who are unable to pull their full weight.

Though the librarian can only advise his staff to gain a detailed knowledge of the book stock, he can and should train them to do all administrative work well. Every new entrant will naturally be made familiar with departmental routine, but something

STAFF

more is needed. When carrying out certain duties, he should be encouraged to exercise good habits of thought and action necessary for their successful performance. Concentration on the job in hand, observation, speed and accuracy in working have little or nothing to do with intellectual capacity; they can become part of the administrative equipment of almost every assistant, provided that the organisation is planned to bring them constantly into action. It is important both for the library and the assistant that they should be acquired. Every library contains great numbers of records which must be accurately kept. It is obviously impossible to make a double check of all work done; moreover, unless all the staff are properly trained, errors will continue, with their deplorable effect on the public service, whatever systems of check are devised. Assistants can so easily become slipshod in their work, and the habit, once formed, is so hard to eradicate, that the librarian owes a duty to his younger staff to compel them to observe strict rules of work while they are still young enough to be malleable. It is an axiom of administration that bad work, undetected, drives out good. Unless every error is brought to the notice of the assistant who has made it, inefficiency will tend to increase; the able members of the staff will be led to believe that their good work remains unnoticed and eventually they will become discouraged and lapse into the ways of their less competent colleagues. The need for absolute accuracy in library processes should be impressed on all new entrants and they should be taught to check all their work until the action becomes automatic; speed can come later.

CHAPTER V

BOOK STOCK

BEFORE the librarian begins to consider his choice of books for the commercial and technical library, he must have his general lines of policy clear. Some librarians, whilst they would not envisage anything less than full student service for the technical library, may prefer to keep the commercial library as an information service only. Where the two sections are administered together, it is logical and more practical to give similar full service in both; if they are kept separate, each may have its own range; but in either case, the decision must be made before book selection is begun.

This is particularly important because the nucleus of a library of this kind is usually composed of books withdrawn from the general reference library, so that the decision must be made in the knowledge that any second thoughts will involve much confusion and extra work, and that in the final rearrangement the general lines of division must be clear to those who normally use either the general or the special libraries. The problems raised by these requirements are rather different in the commercial and the technical sections because subjects which may be considered "commercial" drive much more deeply into the adjacent classes of social science, which are normally the sphere of students of the humanities, than do any of those covered in the technical library. It is therefore more convenient to discuss the stocks of the two sections separately.

THE COMMERCIAL LIBRARY

The selection of books and other material, both as regards type and range, must depend almost wholly on the demand for them. In using the word "demand", it is not suggested that only books which have been asked for should be stocked, for in the special library supply often creates demand. The majority of readers simply do not come again if they find it lacking in what they consider to be essential records. Suggestions for improving the stock are usually only made by readers when they have gained some confidence in the library's value and when the staff have been able to establish friendly and helpful relations with them. In its initial stages, therefore, the library must attempt to anticipate the needs of its readers. Its material can later be adjusted to satisfy their known wants, and this process must be continuous. As all books must be up to date, and the high price and frequent reissue of heavily used books such as directories make the cost of book provision proportionately greater than in the general libraries, careful check should be kept on their use to find whether or not they justify their purchase.

The most important purpose of the commercial

BOOK STOCK

library is to act as a business information bureau. Though few commercial libraries keep records of the use of the quick reference books, or the number of enquiries for information of a factual nature, there can be little doubt that readers who come for such purposes greatly outnumber those who undertake detailed study or research on commercial subjects. This point is mentioned here to emphasise the importance of providing material to answer commercial enquiries in such range and quality (or up-to-dateness) that a high standard of efficiency and accuracy is attained. Whilst librarians assume the responsibility of ensuring, so far as it is possible to do so, that information given by the books they issue in all branches of knowledge should be reliable, the onus of accepting this information rests on the reader. The harm that may be done by a book which is factually inaccurate is rarely measurable in a general library. In a commercial library, on the other hand, much of the information given is of a type that would make error costly to the enquirer; moreover, the source would be known, and the library's prestige would suffer in consequence. Efficient staff service is essential because of the amount of factual information which has to be provided by the staff for enquirers unused to books and sources, but even the most competent assistant is unable to make up for deficiencies in the books. This applies with particular force to quick reference commercial books. A comparatively small selection of current good books of this type is therefore generally more useful than a large stock which has not been kept up to date.

Directories and annuals

Directories are probably the most used books in the commercial library. Those who use them are not as a rule familiar with the use of books as sources of information, and are likely to be impressed when they find that the library can provide definite answers to questions which are often urgent and may be important. From this point of view directories are the special library's equivalent of the "introductory" type of book stocked in lending libraries: they are the ground bait for potentially good library users. Directories should therefore be adequate in range and number, and the latest editions should always be available.

The gaps in the directories published in this and some other countries directly affected by the war have not been filled at the time of writing; and it seems unlikely that they will be for some time to come. Other sources of information have to be found to supplement them, such as telephone directories and annuals, some of which, though not true directories, are nevertheless very useful. Their value depends so much on local needs that there is no point in attempting to give a list of even the more outstanding ones. The librarian must make his choice from the following sources, or examine the large numbers stocked in the libraries of cities with wide commercial interests.

BOOK STOCK

The Directory of Directories, Annuals and Reference Books, 1950. (Business Publications.)

Henderson, G. P., *comp. Current British Directories*, 1953. (Staples.)

Trade lists issued by such firms as Kelly's Directories, Butler's Advertising Services (including Overseas publications) and Vaughan's *List of Directories, Who's Who, Press Guides and Year Books*.

Library Lists, such as those issued by the Cities of London and Westminster Public Libraries, are also helpful, and the invaluable *Guide to Reference Books*, by Constance M. Winchell (American Library Association), based on Mudge's standard work, should be the librarian's constant companion.

Most British directories are published by the well-known firm of Kelly, who issue at intervals lists of those available, though with a saddening number of asterisks denoting volumes out of print. They comprise, first of all, full-scale directories for large towns; these contain official information and sections covering streets, names of residents and professions and trades, each section being arranged alphabetically. It should be noted that in the residential lists only those persons who inhabit premises above a certain standard are included. London is covered by the *Post Office London Directory*. The old Kelly's county directories, planned on somewhat similar lines, have been replaced since the war by over a hundred small local directories of London suburbs, and of provincial towns with their adjacent areas.

COMMERCIAL AND TECHNICAL LIBRARIES

These contain two lists, one of private residents and one of tradesmen.

The next group of home directories is comprised of those dealing with certain industries and trades such as building; chemical industries; leather; watch, clock and jewellery trades, etc. Unfortunately the Kelly's trade directories are all of pre-war vintage, but certain long established ones issued by other firms, such as Ryland's *Coal, Iron, Steel, Engineering and Hardware Industries*, and Worrall's *Yorkshire Textile Industry*, can be obtained in post-war editions. International directories like Kelly's *Directory of Merchants, Manufacturers and Shippers*, and directories of industries published abroad, include British firms. The five issued by Camille Rousset on the chemical, leather, electrical, textile and hardware and metals industries, with an index in four languages, are an example.

A supplementary source is provided by annuals. These are published by agencies such as trade associations and periodicals concerned with certain industries, which produce annual handbooks or supplements. For instance, valuable information can be found in *Cabinet-maker Year Book* (Benn); *Pottery Gazette Reference Book and Directory; British Plastics Year Book* (Iliffe); The *Gas World Year Book* (Benn); *Buyers' Guide* (Supplement to *Chemistry and Industry*); *Shipping World Year Book and Who's Who; British Chemicals and their Manufacturers*, published by the Association of British Chemical Manufacturers, and many others.

BOOK STOCK

From the large number of foreign and commonwealth directories available the librarian must choose, with much selective caution because of their high cost, those most likely to meet the needs of the town's industrial and mercantile interests. Details of them can be obtained from the sources before mentioned. Certain publications, which have almost become standard, such as the Didot-Bottin series (France); *Annuario Generale d'Italia* (Italy); Thacker's *Directory of India and Pakistan;* Thomas's *Register of American Manufacturers* (United States); and *Anuario Kraft* (South America) will probably find a place in any commercial library. During recent years the appearance of several German directories, like the impressive Bequna series, has been welcome. Many industrial and business directories are published in the United States. The November 1952 issue of the Cleveland Public Library *Bulletin* of the Business Information Bureau gives a useful list of them. Mention has already been made of the usefulness of annuals of all kinds and telephone directories; the latter can be obtained for many countries at reasonable prices from the Controller of the Post Office Supplies Department in London.

There are many other records of a special type which may be classed variously as directories, annuals, year books, etc. They list people, organisations and activities, and selection from them can only be made after a careful study of sources. Some, however, are so well known as to merit special mention: the *Directory of Directors;* the *Stock Exchange Year Book;*

COMMERCIAL AND TECHNICAL LIBRARIES

Sell's *Telegraphic Addresses;* Garcke's *Manual of Electricity Supply;* the *Municipal Year Book;* and the *Hospitals Year Book,* for example. The professional directories and registers covering medicine, law, accountancy, dentistry, clergy, surveying, etc., will also probably find a place on the directory shelves.

Some of the annuals, particularly those published by periodicals dealing with industries, may not be found in directory lists. In view of the scarcity of good directories in Britain, the librarian should keep a careful watch for such publications and subscribe to the periodicals which issue them. His sources of directory information can be greatly extended at a comparatively small cost in this way. They are also useful as records of trade marks and trade names.

In dealing with annuals in this section emphasis has been placed on those which serve, even in part, the purpose of a directory and would naturally be shelved with them. There are many other annuals of different kinds: year books of societies and organisations which record the year's work in certain fields of study, or conference papers and similar material; those issued yearly by national and international organisations; and the records of professional and technical bodies. These will probably be shelved with the normal stock of the library.

Telegraphic codes

No fewer than 98 different telegraphic codes are on stock in public commercial libraries, the largest number in any one library being 54. The libraries

BOOK STOCK

of the mercantile and seaport cities naturally make the most generous provision of them.

It has been suggested that as most firms have their own copies of the codes they normally use, and list them on their letter-heads, there is not much point in the library providing them as well. The fact that in most libraries codes are well used suggests that many smaller firms do not possess copies of those in common use and that even the largest business houses are sometimes faced with the problem of decoding messages based on one of the lesser known systems.

Every commercial library should provide some of the popular codes, such as the *A.B.C.*; *Bentley's*; *Marconi International*; *Rudolf-Mosse*; and *Western Union*, the first two of which are in considerable demand. Beyond this minimum, the librarian has a wide range of choice which might well be based on the number of requests received. The nature of the town's business interests will, of course, influence the selection of special codes. Seaports will require such records as *Boe Commercial Phrase and Shipping Code*; *Lombard Shipping and Transport Code*; *Scott's Code*; the *Shipowners' Telegraphic Code*, or others of like nature. Industrial centres, according to the kind of products they make, will probably stock such codes as the *Beama Technical Cable Code* (British Electrical and Allied Manufacturers' Association); *Bentley's Wool Supplement*; *Buenting's International Cotton Code*; *McNeill's Code for Mining, Metallurgical and Civil Engineers*; *Selwyn's International Chemical Code*

COMMERCIAL AND TECHNICAL LIBRARIES

and *International Telegraphic Code for the Iron and Steel Trades; Textile Cable Code; Zebra Wood Code,* and so on.

Whereas, in the case of directories, the librarian has to limit their numbers because they are costly and must be renewed at short intervals, he may safely work on an opposite principle in buying codes. Though supplements are sometimes issued, codes do not "date" quickly: they are like dictionaries of language in always having a possible use, whatever their age. The first cost is often the only cost, and the librarian may therefore feel justified in providing a reasonable range of them even though some may only rarely be used.

Time tables

An adequate range of rail, road and air time tables should be stocked. The regional guides of British Railways can all be obtained free. *Bradshaw* and the *London A.B.C.* should also find a place, together with any local *A.B.C.* or other guides. For the continent, *Bradshaw's Continental Guide* is the best known, but *Cook's Continental Time Table* may be preferred because it is cheaper. The *Continental Time Table* of British Railways is useful for main line routes with connections from London. These should be sufficient to cover the needs of most library users.

The growth in the use of the roads for long distance journeys makes it necessary to provide information about coach and bus services. The *A.B.C.*

Coach Guide, published three times a year, gives time tables and fares for long distance express routes, with a selection of local bus services which usefully connect with them. For other bus guides it is necessary to approach the individual companies.

Bradshaw's International Air Guide, issued monthly gives full details of air lines throughout the world. The somewhat similar *Official Airline Guide* is published monthly in Chicago, U.S.A.

The librarian should watch for the publication of new guides to travel by air and road as these services are rapidly expanding.

Trade catalogues

To answer the common question, "What firm makes a particular type of article?" catalogues of the products made by manufacturers should be collected and adequately indexed. Producing firms are always willing to send their catalogues and to keep the issues current; the librarian's main difficulty is to fix a reasonable limit to the number he can accept. Only experience of their use and the requests received for others can guide his choice, but he will probably find it best to begin his collection with the catalogues of the large and well-known firms, both home and foreign, concerned with products used locally.

Maps and plans

No rules can be laid down about the number

COMMERCIAL AND TECHNICAL LIBRARIES

and kind of maps and plans which should be stocked. A few standard atlases should certainly be provided. Some librarians find it advisable to take from the directories all town plans which can be removed and file them apart; such plans, folded, are easily stored, occupy little space, and are always useful. There need be no limit to the size of the collection. Large maps, on the other hand, are costly, as are the methods of mounting and storing them. Here again, use and demand are the determining factors: the seaport towns will naturally provide far more than the industrial towns, which usually find that the atlases serve all reasonable needs. A collection of plans of docks of British and foreign ports has also been found helpful in the commercial libraries of seaports.

The main book stock

Most of the books and other material described in the previous pages are heavily used by readers, and they will probably be placed apart from the main sequence on special shelving near the entrance. From this point the main stock of the commercial library may be mixed with that of the technical library. This would ensure that books useful in both sections—for example, in some sub-divisions of class 331—would not be overlooked; on the other hand, not all the books constituting the commercial library would be immediately apparent. The Dewey classification, which is found in so many British libraries that it is used as the basis of discussion through-

BOOK STOCK

out, mixes certain subjects usually considered "commercial" and "technical"—for example, books on business methods are classified in 650, a technical sub-division—so, if the layout of the room is suitable and there are sound administrative reasons for doing so, the books may be separated into two divisions, each with its own Dewey sequence. Neither course is decisively better than the other.

The librarian must make up his own mind what subjects his commercial library is intended to cover. His final decision will be influenced partly by his understanding of the fields of knowledge concerned and the needs of readers, partly by such practical considerations as the nature of the available premises, the arrangement and scope of the other departments of the library, and the funds at his disposal. The choice will, however, largely be determined by the answer to a basic question: is the library stock to represent "commerce" as a field of knowledge, or to provide material of practical value to the business community only?

To embark upon the creation of a library of the first type, serving business man, student, historian, general enquirer, and all other possible users, is not so easy as it appears at first sight. There is no part of the Dewey classification in which a group of subjects suitable for a library of this kind appears as such; the only scheme, in fact, which could confidently be used as a guide for coverage is that drawn up by the Library of Congress, in whose classification Sections HD to HJ have been compiled with care to bring into logical juxtaposition all the past and present-day factors which affect the economic and commercial state of the world. But this is a scheme designed for an advanced research library aiming at completeness, in which an informational or selective service is of secondary importance and no account is taken of "user-interest". The tables sweep into their net, for instance, economic history from the most ancient times, and exhaustive lists of labour topics which are properly social and political studies. Carried to this logical conclusion, a department having books on the trade relations between India and Imperial Rome, accounting methods in Assyria and the leisure pursuits of the modern working classes, *The Journey to Work* and all the Utopian economic planning schemes of the 1940's, would be too large and too scholarly to be run as part of the commercial library; it would bring in students not really interested in commercial activities as such, and in many cases requiring so many books from other departments that service would be complicated by the constant passing of books from one to another. Students of economic and commercial history nearly always work in a mental environment of general history. Moreover, there would arise a very real conflict of principle. It has already been said that the main consideration in book selection for the commercial library must be to take demand and use as guides; but if the library is to cater for serious students of recondite subjects it must be prepared to stock many important books which can only be in occasional demand, on the principle that "a good reference library must have it". In this connection it is of interest to note that in one library, with long and successful experience in the administration of a commercial department, it has been thought advisable to reorganise the service by transferring the books suitable for the student of commerce to the general reference library, and making the commercial library purely an information service.

Nevertheless, the librarian may, if he has space and need for so large a special library, think it advisable to keep all subjects related to commerce, communications, finance and economics together; in which case it is enough to say that he will choose for the commercial library all books which can be suitably classified in Dewey's sections, 310, 330–334, 336–338, parts of 340, 380 and the sub-divisions of 650 which specifically relate to business methods, with the appropriate bibliographical divisions of class 000, and commercial and economic geographies.

If the library is meant to serve the current needs of business men and workers in practical fields, certain sub-divisions of Dewey can be lifted from the tables and the stock confined to those books clearly classifiable within them. Border-line cases can be decided by the reader-interest test, the more easily as it is almost always possible for the classifier to find an alternative number in Dewey—a scheme distinguished by a useful vagueness of outlook—

which would bring a particular book within the classes represented in the general reference library. In a few classes, notably parts of 331 and 380, the line of division between the two departments cannot be kept clear by Dewey sub-numbers; there will have to be some in each department bearing the same number, but distinguished from one another by reader-interest. A reader is not likely to go into a "commercial" library for *Domesday Book* because the classifier has put it at 336.42.

The librarian who decides to limit the commercial section to current needs must keep a continual check on the growth of the stock to make sure that it serves its avowed purpose and does not become a mongrel. Departmental librarians always have an expansionist tendency because they naturally dislike saying "we haven't got it". This is particularly to be kept in mind in the case of files of serials and periodicals. Whilst files for a few years are needed for purely informational work, there will come a point when they have lengthened so far that they are useful only to the scholar, and will become unbalanced in relation to the rest of the stock. This can be prevented by transferring them to the general reference library, or discarding them after an agreed number of years. This matter should be decided with some care when a new serial is added to the stock, as it is all too easy both to harbour useless material and to regret discards with some bitterness. The test should rather be whether the information given in the files can be obtained elsewhere than

BOOK STOCK

whether the recent issues have been much used, as in the case of historical material demand cannot be anticipated.

The paragraphs below list the subjects which it is essential to cover in the commercial library, with some notes on classification. These subjects are presented as minimum requirements; other classes can be drawn in according to the views and circumstances of the individual librarian. The Dewey numbers given are those of the 14th edition except where direct reference is made to the 15th edition.

(a) Bibliographies and catalogues of libraries on the subjects covered.

(b) Books dealing with economic conditions, statistic, current or recent surveys of commerce, industry, trade, finance, living conditions affecting the visiting merchant, markets, resources, products, etc., divided by countries.

A certain amount of confusion can arise here. If such books are classified at a sub-division of 310, it may puzzle readers if the theory of statistics and demography are placed in another department; while some will seem to the classifier to be correctly placed at 330·9, in which case they will be confused with books on economic history shelved in the reference library. A good way to provide a clear-cut line between the two departments is to place all books classified at 310–313 and all those at 330·9 in the general reference library, and to classify all economic and commercial surveys at 314–319. If this practice is adopted, the public will find all recent information about a country at the one number. The *China Year Book* and the Department of Overseas

COMMERCIAL AND TECHNICAL LIBRARIES

Trade's *Survey of Economic Conditions in China* will be together in the commercial library; Sun Yat Sen's *International Development of China*, an exercise in planning by a political leader, and Tawney's *Land and Labour in China* will be at 330·951 in the reference library.

c. Trade, commerce and communications.

Dewey has, of course, a full division with this title, and at first sight it would seem simple to put everything at 380 in the commercial library. There is, however, room for disagreement here, as nearly everywhere. Few librarians would regard philately (383·22) as a suitable subject for the commercial library; and a case can be made for regarding the history of roads and sea-routes (as distinct from road-making and navigation) as of general historical, rather than commercial, interest. To histories of commerce, and of such bodies as the great trading companies of the 17th and 18th centuries, the points mentioned in pp. 137–8 must apply. The librarian must therefore classify and allocate his books according to user-interest.

(d) Books on the working population and their employers, in so far as they deal with matters arising within the place of work, are of equal interest to merchants and manufacturers. They are suggested for the commercial rather than the technical library because wages, hours of work, etc., affect prices, output and ultimately markets. They are also of use to the general public asking questions affecting their own economic welfare, to whom a commercial library naturally seems to deal with money, insurance, etc. The specific subjects which seem to belong to the commercial library are: wages, cost of living;

social insurance, workmen's compensation (if the 15th edition of Dewey is used these two subjects will be sub-divisions of 368), superannuation, arbitration and conciliation machinery within the factory (but not the trade union itself, which links up with other subjects in the general reference library); discipline (within the organisation); hours of work, safety, hygiene, industrial education, special conditions for particular types of worker.

All these will be classified at various sub-divisions of 331·1–331·8. All books treating the lower income groups as part of the community—social surveys, housing, living conditions, standard of living, demography, etc.—are better in the general library, where they are shelved with social care, delinquency, education, historical background, crime, justice, and other subjects dealing with man in society.

(e) The study of business method is also common to commerce and industry. Office methods (building, equipment, organisation, administration, files and correspondence); writing, typewriting, shorthand; book-keeping, accountancy, costing; industrial management (finance, retail shop management, buying and selling); advertising and public relations; are the subjects covered by the sub-division of 650, which would be a class easily lifted out from the technical library were it not for the awkward intrusion of 655, which is a table for the technical books on printing, and 654 and 656, which are better merged, as is recommended in the 15th edition of Dewey, in 383–388 and 621.38.

COMMERCIAL AND TECHNICAL LIBRARIES

(f) The sub-divisions of 332 and 336 (banking, building societies, pawnbroking, money and exchange, investment, credit, interest, public finance, taxation) present no difficulty, except that books on such matters in ancient and mediæval times should go to the general reference library in accordance with the principles already outlined.

(g) Insurance, classified by Dewey at 368, can be placed without difficulty in the commercial library.

(h) The only subject in the 350's which might usefully be found in the commercial library is local government finance (352.1), which is likely to interest the same type of reader as accountancy and taxation. If the practice of the 15th edition of Dewey is followed, and everything related to rating placed at 336.28, no difficulty arises. All the other subjects in 350 relate to government as such and are better in the general library.

(i) Whether any books on law are included in the department must largely depend on local practice. There is certainly a case for having those dealing with the companies acts, advertising, trade marks, employers' liability and such subjects in it; but if all legal text-books have always been shelved in the general reference library, there are equally strong arguments for keeping them together there, since law as a subject is one of the humanities. If it is thought advisable to divide them, Dewey's action in singling out, in parts of class 347, some aspects of law of special interest to the business community, may be followed by placing the following divisions in the commercial library: 347.2 (real property); 347.3 (chattels, including sale); 347.4 (contracts); and 347.7 (commercial and maritime law).

The number 347.9 (civil trials, procedure) as treated in Dewey is of little help to the public librarian, probably because it was drawn up by an American. County courts, for instance, which are of modern foundation and whose business is largely concerned with financial and industrial disputes, have no obvious place in the table; 347.99 is usually filled by classifiers with a medley of historical matter on manor courts, wards and liveries, Star Chamber, forest courts, and similar organisations quite remote from commercial or even modern legal concern. The other places (347.91 to 347.98, on duties of justices, procedure, law of evidence, etc.) would logically be found in the general reference library. The librarian will probably find it easier to put all this class there and, if he thinks it necessary to have a section on county courts and civil suits in the commercial library, to invent a special number for them.

Books of an encyclopædic nature such as Halsbury's *Laws of England*, Halsbury's or Chitty's *Statutes* or the *Public General Acts*, and law lexicons such as Wharton's or Burrows's *Words and Phrases judicially defined*, are equally well placed in any of the reference libraries. The decision might well be governed by the proportion of other legal works in one or other departments, or by the purely practical consideration of easy accessibility, as they are mainly used for quick reference.

The *Statutory Instruments* are in even heavier demand than the encyclopaedic works, and much the same arguments can be used for placing them in one or the other of the departments. Where there is an information bureau dealing with questions of a personal and social kind, it will probably be found best to divide them by subject, as about a third of them can with advantage be used there. The rest are so largely concerned with matters such as prices, conditions of import, agricultural procedure, etc., directly affecting the business man that if it is thought undesirable to split them, their proper place is in the commercial library. Much must depend on local conditions (for instance, in many places social welfare questions are dealt with in the general reference library), and the decision taken with regard to the statute law in general. It is essential that the whole series should be easily available, whether together or separately, if enquiries are to be answered quickly and accurately. It should be noted that so many lists and indexes have to be issued to guide the staff through their complicated amendments and cancellations that they are more easily administered if kept together.

(j) Financial rights and dues, the law and practice relating to them, and the different ways in which industrial and private enterprises may be financed, are subjects dealt with by Dewey in ways which indicate no sharp division between a commercial and a general library. For instance, 333 represents the different ways of dealing with land, but many books commonly classified at 333.1, .2, .3, .7 deal with older forms of economy—open field farming, manorial rights, 18th century enclosure, royal forest, arguments about the ownership of land as the key to a régime or political reform—which are of no interest to the enquirer for present-day information.

Co-operation, put by Dewey at 334, has wide political and social meanings, but there are books on the actual working of agricultural or industrial co-operative finance which the business man may require. Free trade and protection (337) represent policies affecting the whole national life; but except when his balance of mind is upset by political excitements, the trader is only interested in the actual duties currently imposed. It is therefore suggested that the commercial library as here envisaged should stock the following range of books in the classes 333, 334 and 337: 333.5 rent of land for cultivation; 333.6 rent of land for building, general works on rent; 333.8 mines; 333.9 water and air rights; 334.1 building societies; 334.2 to 334.6 co-operative banks, insurance, stores, factories, etc., from the point of view of internal administration and finance only; 337.4 subsidies; 337.5 duties on special articles; 337.6 duties on raw materials (books explaining the scales in operation, not arguments for and against). Some of these subjects are modified in a helpful way in the 15th edition of Dewey, but the outlook is still predominantly American.

COMMERCIAL AND TECHNICAL LIBRARIES

(k) Finally, the selector approaches the subject of industrial organisation, which Dewey puts at 338, divided illogically partly by nature of product and partly by forms of organisation. The librarian in charge of books of current and useful information must consider user-interest almost entirely in this section, and the arguments already outlined concerning commercial and industrial history must be examined carefully here. Are people who use a business library really interested in the organisation of the guilds merchant in the fifteenth century? In cases of doubt, a good test is: does the book help the industrial organiser, or does it seek to set the industry into the general pattern of the country's history? By this test, Ashton's *Iron and Steel in the Industrial Revolution* is a history book; it seeks mainly to show what effect the industry had on the development of England at that day, and how the people then developed the industry. Andrew and Brunner's *Capital Development in Steel*, on the other hand, is a study of present-day problems of moment to all senior officials and owners of businesses. A book on Big Business "as a power" should have a political number, not be shelved with books on the finance of running or forming a combine. Histories of individual firms and particular techniques are more properly in the province of the technical library and will be dealt with later.

With these factors borne in mind, the following sub-divisions are suggested for the commercial library: 338.1 to 338.4 books on the organisation, productive capacity, etc., of the industries listed; 338.5 books on prices, current finance; 338.7 to 338.9 corporate industries, monopolies, industrial legislation: current description and discussion.

English-foreign dictionaries of commercial terms, and such commercial and economic geographies as are of use to the normal commercial user should also be included in the stock.

THE TECHNICAL LIBRARY

The technical library will require a wide range of scientific and technical dictionaries, English-foreign and foreign-English. The librarian may find it necessary to buy every good one published, because such dictionaries are much used, the staff frequently have difficulty in identifying the needed word, and new terms are constantly appearing as research and production advance. He should certainly not omit Pitman's *Technical Dictionary of Engineering and Industrial Science in seven Languages*, by Ernest Slater and others, or *Technologische Wörterbuch*, originally by Egbert von Hoyer and Franz Kreuter, edited by A. Schlomann (English, French and German); and he should remember that a great number of enquiries will be for words in Portuguese, Russian, and other less well-known languages.

One of the main services of this library will be to help in tracking down books, and even more frequently periodical articles, on certain subjects in which the local industries have developed specialised interests. Some subjects, being clearly of outstanding importance, will be bibliographically covered at the outset; in other cases, the librarian must be on the alert to notice tendencies in current research so as to ensure that his bibliographical aids will be equal to any demands likely to be made on them. The development of fabrics woven of glass fibre, for instance, would stimulate an unwonted interest in glass technology in a textile town. He must also note that certain subjects which appear, at first sight, to bear little relation to one another, often interlock in books. It may not be immediately apparent, for example, that the student of refractories for metallurgical use can find basic information on clays in books on ceramics.

The acquisition of bibliographies on these subjects is an obvious step. Periodical indexes are perhaps of even more importance. The *Engineering Index* and the *Industrial Arts Index*, both American cumulated publications, should be found in any technical library. The former indexes a wide range of periodicals from many countries; the value of the *Industrial Arts Index*, though its subject coverage is broad, is somewhat restricted by the heavy preponderance of American journals among the much smaller number it analyses. Both carry the latest printed information procurable and between them cover a wide field. They can be supplemented by the Library Association *Subject Index to Periodicals*, but as this is published only in annual volumes, it cannot be used for current material.

Next come the many series of abstracts available.

Some, dealing with basic science, such as *Chemical Abstracts* (American Chemical Society) and the separate or expanded series which are now carrying on the work of the discontinued *British Abstracts*, should certainly always be stocked. It may also be thought desirable to have the well-known *Chemisches Zentralblatt* and the broader based *Bulletin Analytique*. Complete sets of those relating to local industries should be provided. Some, such as *British Ceramic Abstracts*, *Baking Abstracts* or *Lace Research Bulletin*, would obviously only be useful in certain libraries, but others which come fairly frequently into the field of enquiry should be added.

Selection of subjects for the technical library is simpler than in the commercial library in that specific sub-divisions of the classification readily declare their right of inclusion; for instance, it is easy to decide that everything classified at 670 and its sub-divisions should go in. But before the choice is made, it is as essential to decide on aim, size and subject coverage as it is in the case of the commercial library.

The aim will almost certainly be to serve the general needs of the advanced student and the technician and, in the local industries or other special interests, the research worker. Elementary text-books, unless they contain information not otherwise obtainable, will not be stocked.

The size of the library and its subject coverage are, of course, closely interrelated, as in a library intended for the student any limitation will be in the subjects and not in the number of books carried in each of them. The librarian's first task will be to decide what, within the limits of the space available, he is to call "technology". Is he to include everything designated by Dewey "useful arts" and transfer the whole of the 600 class? Or is he to confine himself to those industrial and engineering subjects which are the concern of people normally thought of as technicians? In the latter case, he will probably exclude medicine and the domestic sciences, and possibly agriculture; for though the modern farmer needs electrical and mechanical appliances, he is no more a mechanic than the radiologist who interprets an X-ray film is a photographer.

Such a decision is not enough in itself; a department containing only books classified in the 600's would not satisfy the industrial research worker. The older academic names of the useful arts as applied or mechanic *sciences* express a fact, and a century ago it was relatively easy to recognise and apply a distinction between pure and applied science. Then technicians were primarily engaged in perfecting the actual construction and working principles of machines, but the gap between their work and that of the pure scientist has been narrowing rapidly in proportion to the increasing speed with which the discoveries of the laboratory worker are being taken up by the industrialist or the engineer. Though the scientist, intent on his search for knowledge in itself, may have little interest in the use made of his discoveries, others eagerly seek to apply them; indeed, an increasing proportion of scientists now actually work for those whose business it is to do so. In the provincial universities, too, the relations between scientists and industry are close. The more advanced the technical processes, the more closely the findings of the pure scientist are involved in their evolution. There are technical studies in which propositions can only be clearly stated in terms of mathematical formulæ; and the intrusion of physics into research and experiments which ultimately find expression in industrial processes has become increasingly evident during recent years. These trends are affecting the way in which advanced technical books are being written, and subjects which previously appeared to be quite distinct are being linked up in books.[1] It is becoming more and more difficult for the librarian to separate books on pure and applied science in certain fields, and in trying to make sure that related books are together, he will find himself transferring many whole classes to the commercial and technical library. This inevitably leads him to consider whether it is wise to try to make any distinction between science and technology, since, if any attempt is made to do so, the number of books left in the other departments of the main library may often be less than those transferred.

It will also be found in practice that the separation of those scientific books which might reason-

[1] "The dividing line between pure and applied science is so fast becoming nebulous that the American Chemical Society has combined its two editorial boards and issues one volume on a particular subject for all purposes and all users." *Food Manufacture*, Vol. 28, 1953, p. 395.

ably fit into the librarian's concept of "technology" may cause a great deal of confusion among readers. However carefully subjects and individual books are chosen, there must always be occasions when some of them seem to be in the wrong library. Sensible administration and co-operation between the various departments in the main building can overcome many of the resulting difficulties; but if, for any reason, the special library is placed elsewhere, much duplication of important and costly books is needed. As in all subjects theory and practice imperceptibly merge, it will probably be thought best, in the interest both of readers and library administration, to recognise the futility of attempts to separate them and transfer all scientific as well as technical books to the department.

It will be noted that *all* books on science are meant, and not merely those sciences which have industrial technical applications. If the subject groupings in the new library are wide and inclusive, there will be fewer difficulties in administration.

In the foregoing argument it has been assumed that if he decides to have a science and technology library, the librarian will simply transfer to the new department the whole of the 500 and 600 classes of Dewey. It may be, however, that he has decided, as was suggested earlier, to omit medicine (610), agriculture (630) and domestic science (640). In that case, he will find it easy, if he so desires, to exclude three sciences—botany, zoology and biology —which as the study of living organisms provide the natural facts on which these human practices are based.

Selection is not, of course, really as simple as this. Once his basic stock is agreed upon, the librarian will find himself up against many little problems both about subjects and individual books, and might just as well solve them by his personal views as otherwise. For instance, it has already been suggested that the 650 class, with the exception of printing, be put in the commercial library as of interest both to traders and manufacturers; but it may be thought preferable to keep printing in the commercial library on the same grounds, and have the advantage of shelving a whole class together.

Another decision involving the 650 class will probably be made according to local conditions. Subjects classified without apparent alternative by Dewey in the 700 class are those branches of drawing, lettering and design which are the province of the poster-artist, the man in charge of advertisement layout, and the colour printer. A works' publicity manager must know something of all of them; but the man who draws a poster or designs a brochure cover is primarily an artist, who will usually look for books on his subject in the general reference library. If, as is likely, there is a school of art in the neighbourhood, it is better to keep all books on the graphic arts, including those meant for commercial designers, together in the appropriate sections of the 700 class. If there is no such school, the number of books needed will be fewer and more directly related to the needs of persons actually employed as commercial artists, and might be classified at 659; in which case, if the commercial and technical sections of the library are kept separate, they will be shelved in the commercial library. The present writer's preference, in normal circumstances, is for keeping all books on the principles of the graphic arts together in the 700 class; it is not easy to draw a line between art and its applications.

Many similar difficulties will arise with other subjects, such as photography. As no question of principle is involved, the librarian should base his decision on his own judgment and the practical needs of his library and its readers.

Certain kinds of publications essential to the technical library are dealt with in more detail below.

Government publications

British government publications are announced by Her Majesty's Stationery Office in daily, monthly and annual lists; and in this very large field of basic literature there is so much that is essential that some chief librarians have attempted to solve the problems of selection and supply by placing a standing order for everything issued, allocating the documents to suitable departments as they come. The output is, however, very large, and includes many series of purely administrative interest; a few years of such collecting results in a considerable unnecessary expenditure of money, and the time spent in sorting

BOOK STOCK

and the space used in storing many of them are also wasted in a public library. The only real advantage of the all-in standing order is that delivery is immediate—a matter of some importance in cities where there is no branch of the Stationery Office—but it is generally possible to decide on a large range of annual and series standing orders which will be promptly delivered, and to obviate some of the delay with non-serial items by using H.M.S.O.'s conveniently designed order form as soon as the daily lists arrive. Telegraphic ordering when the notices about important reports appear in the leading newspapers on the day of publication can be used in special cases. The Stationery Office does not print or sell the publications of the nationalised industries, and there are some small publications, such as the Department of Scientific and Industrial Research's *Translated Contents List of Russian Periodicals*, which do not appear in the lists. How to find out about these extra publications is discussed exhaustively by the contributors to *Government Information and the Research Worker*, edited by Ronald Staveley (Library Association, 1952). Other aspects of the search for government publications, including the problem of finding copies of older ones, are dealt with in R. D. Roberts's *Introduction to Reference Books*, 1948. There is no list of items still in print, so that even a careful search of H.M.S.O.'s sectional and departmental lists is no guarantee that a copy of the desired item can be acquired. The departmental lists are not very

COMMERCIAL AND TECHNICAL LIBRARIES

old, and for bibliographical enquiries such publications as P. S. King and Son's *Catalogue of Parliamentary Publications*, 1800–1900, with two supplements to 1920, should be used. The Inter-departmental Committee on Social and Economic Research is planning a series of guides to sources, of which three—*Labour Statistics, Censuses of Britain,* 1801–1931, and *Local Government Statistics*—have so far appeared. In many cases the librarian will find himself falling back on the long files of the *Cumulative Book Index*, Whitaker's *Cumulative Book Lists* and *Reference Catalogue of Current Literature*, the *English Catalogue of Books*, and the other normal sources of book selection.

The United States Government, probably the largest publisher in the world, issues a *Monthly Catalog*. A guide through the maze of departments and sub-departments is provided by A. M. Boyd's *United States Government Publications*, revised by R. E. Rips in 1949. It describes the relationship of the departments, and the sort of material each publishes. A fair selection of United States government publications appears in the *Cumulative Book Index*, and many of these which are really of interest to the British public are mentioned in the usual sources of book selection.

The United Nations Organisation issues each month, through its Department of Public Information, *Documents Index: United Nations and Specialised Agencies Documents and Publications*. It is sold by H.M.S.O.

BOOK STOCK

Societies

Public libraries should be members of all institutions carrying out work bearing on their specialised subjects. Apart from their journals or transactions, societies often issue information and ephemeral material which is up to date and authoritative, and some of them sponsor valuable text-books. Subscriptions to American societies are particularly helpful because it is not always easy to obtain their new publications quickly if they are ordered through the normal channels and they often allow favourable discounts to members.

Sponsored publications

A considerable number of scientific and technical works are being produced by private firms in addition to those published under the authority of societies and university presses. Many handbooks concerned with shop practice and other matters are compiled by competent technicians employed by larger organisations, and being officially sponsored by them, are often more practical and valuable than the normal text-book, which has not to pass so searching a test. Others deal with the production and processing of certain materials, and have outstanding value. The librarian should watch for these in the routine checks of reviews and announcements in periodicals. Some are offered free in regular lists in periodicals (in the case of American firms in, for instance, *Iron Age* and *Steel*); occasionally it requires a carefully worded request to secure a copy; others are offered for sale and advertised in suitable periodicals—the book on *Fan Engineering* issued by the firm of Woods of Colchester is a good example.

Standard specifications

One of the most frequent and important types of practical enquiry is for copies of standard specifications and similar "footrule" publications. The position with regard to their publication is somewhat complicated.

In Britain a government assisted body, the British Standards Institute, issues specifications for minimum standards for nearly every type of product and undertaking. Librarians of large libraries who take out full subscriptions are supplied with all the specifications; their names, listed in the institute's *Yearbook*, show users where a whole series can be consulted. Several official bodies, such as British Railways and some other government controlled undertakings, make their own standards. Apart from official issues of this type, specifications are printed by private firms for their staffs' guidance when fulfilling contracts, and the librarian should be on the watch for any information about such of them as deal with subjects in which the library specialises.

In the United States the official body, the National Bureau of Standards, is an establishment of the Department of Commerce. On request, and in accordance with its own programme, it carries out tests in all the sciences except the biological, and undertakes research calculated to produce acceptable standards of measurement of pressure, velocity, electricity, etc., and to eliminate waste and duplication in industry. It also acts as a clearing house of technical information. Its publications are laboratory reports and suggestion handbooks rather than minimum standards in the sense of the British body's publications. In the United States, on the Continent and in the Dominions, the functions of the British body are carried out by private societies (such as the American Society for Testing Materials and Deutscher Normenausschuss), private firms, and by industries collectively (for instance, Bureau de Normes de l'Automobile). Indian Railways, and similar official undertakings, issue their own standards, many of which are useful in technical libraries and should be sought for when there are gaps in the information available in the library. A list of foreign standard making bodies is issued by the British Standards Institute.

Translations

The provision of translations of current foreign papers, generally articles in periodicals, is a matter for library co-operation rather than a problem of book selection. As soon as important items are noticed in foreign journals, research workers in many fields want translations of them. In institutions and large firms translating is usually done on the spot, but students and others will come to the library.

COMMERCIAL AND TECHNICAL LIBRARIES

In places where an interchange organisation, or some similar form of liaison, can be established, the loan between members of translations made by any one of them will be an important part of the service. Copies of translations made further afield, or loans if photocopying is not possible, can only take place at present through the agency of an index kept at the headquarters of ASLIB, which has the inevitable disadvantage of many contributory indexes that it is about two years behindhand. The Department of Scientific and Industrial Research issues a *Translated Contents List of Russian Periodicals* (duplicated) each month.

In the United States, indexes are made by several organisations, such as the Consultants' Bureau in New York, where the index is only about a year behindhand, and arrangements are made for the purchase of issues and reprints. Translations of all articles listed in *Engineering Index* can be bought from the Engineering Society Library, New York. Lists of translations on sale in the field of metallurgy are issued by Henry Brutcher of Altadena, California. The Science Museum Library sells photocopies of many translations from Russian periodicals.

The librarian can only be guided in the choice of translations by his readers' enquiries and suggestions, and will rarely be able to obtain translations of very recent material (which are usually most in demand) except in his own district; but many important papers will, of course, be of use even if they are not

BOOK STOCK

heard of until some suggestion sends him to ASLIB's index.

Abstracts

It has already been suggested that all technical librarians need complete sets of abstracts in certain fields. Abstracts can be chosen from the Royal Society's *List of Periodicals and Bulletins containing Abstracts in Great Britain*, 1950, which gives useful particulars of the number of abstracts included and the extent of the indexing. United States and other foreign abstracts may be found by careful search through Ulrich's *Periodicals Directory*, published by R. H. Bowker Company, and a joint publication of UNESCO and the International Federation for Documentation, *Index Bibliographicus; Directory of Current Periodicals, Abstracts, Bibliographies, Vol.* 1, *Science and Technology* (1951). ASLIB is to undertake a revision of this volume.

Atomic energy reports

Nuclear physics is a subject which has proved to be of interest and value in many departments of research, and the technical librarian will find it necessary to be able to tell many types of enquirers where such publications as the unclassified and declassified reports of the United States Atomic Energy Commission may be seen or borrowed. Copies are deposited at the Science Library, Science Museum, London, and the Science and Commerce Library, Sheffield City Libraries, which will lend

COMMERCIAL AND TECHNICAL LIBRARIES

them on request. The Commission has lately begun to send out some reports in the form of microcards, which will restrict their use to those places where there is a microcard reader.

The corresponding reports of the Atomic Energy Research Establishment can be purchased from H.M.S.O., and may also be borrowed from Sheffield. The reports issued by Atomic Energy of Canada Limited are also now being received at Sheffield and will be lent on request.

BOOK SELECTION IN THE COMMERCIAL AND TECHNICAL LIBRARY

New books

The special department created, as it usually is, by removing certain sections from an established reference library, will already have a sufficiently good basic stock to obviate the necessity of making prolonged searches in bibliographies. Many of the standard lists in the fast developing fields of science and technology are now becoming tools of bibliographical or historical, rather than current, research. The librarian in search of ideas for filling apparent gaps in his basic stock will, of course, check Bestermann's *World Bibliography of Bibliographies* for lists on particular subjects; Bestermann's headings are very specific, but his lists include only separately published works. The Wilson *Bibliographic Index* is up to date and cumulative. Bibliographies of special subjects, including periodical articles and privately printed material, are often announced quite obscurely and should be constantly sought in periodicals, society reports and bulletins, etc. Apart from these standard aids to book selection, the librarian will do best to concentrate on the sources from which he can select new books or new editions.

The book on approval is even more useful to the technical than to the general librarian. There are booksellers who specialise in acquiring a wide range of technical books, including American publications, quickly, and such a bookshop should be visited regularly and books chosen for careful assessment in the library.

The *British National Bibliography*, after the experience of several years, has become a check-list particularly useful to the special librarian. He may not use, and indeed may violently disagree with, its over-elaborate classification, but he can check particular sections with an ease and thoroughness he could not achieve with the older alphabetical lists. Titles dealing with his own preoccupations will be under his notice almost immediately after publication, and those of limited interest issued privately or by small publishing houses frequently meet his eye in the *British National Bibliography* before they are overwhelmed in the spate of present-day printing. The *Catalogue of Lewis's Medical, Scientific and Technical Library*, the Department of Scientific and Industrial Research's *Libraries* (monthly), the ASLIB *Bulletin*, and lists such as the New York Public Library's *New Technical Books*, though too late to use for current buying, are useful in checking for omissions.

The assessment of new publications, however, is largely a matter for the experts who review in periodicals. The first essential for good technical book selection is to take the right journals, and the range of periodicals must be constantly strengthened by the double test of use by the public and the standing of their reviews. The librarian, who cannot be an expert in more than a fraction of the fields he covers, must be ready to seek and accept expert advice on books wherever and whenever he can. He will probably find that about half the periodicals he chooses for the department will contain reliable reviews, and should check them carefully as a regular routine.

Scientific, Industrial and Technical Books published in the United States of America, 1930–1944: Titles in Print with Annotations, was issued in 1946 by the National Research Council's Committee on Bibliography of American Scientific and Technical Books; it has been kept up to date by a supplement published in 1947, by yearly lists in the *Library Journal* each May, and by a supplement to 1952, which has just appeared. This excellent source is naturally affected by the usual time lag. The *Cumulative Book Index* and the *Bibliography of Technical Reports* issued monthly by the United States Department of Commerce, Office of Technical Services (*"PB" Reports*), give more recent information; but the advance notices and catalogues of American scientific and technical publishers, such as Elsevier, McGraw-Hill, Penton, Reinhold, Van Nostrand and Wiley, the booksellers' shelves, and the reviews in periodicals, are the best sources for American books.

Many important United States publications are technical reports direct to authorities responsible for the research they describe and are often most desirable to have but difficult to find. The "PB" list mentioned above is one source; a valuable article by John E. Woolston, *American Technical Reports and how to obtain them*, on the agencies through which they can be found and acquired, appeared in the *Journal of Documentation* for December, 1953.

In this field it is even less profitable than in others to suggest that book selection can be carried out by rule. No text-book lore can help the technical librarian who, like all special librarians, must find his own way about and develop his own flairs.

Replacements

The selection of replacements presents some problems. It is particularly important in this department that all information offered should be the latest available; whilst this is an ideal to be striven for in all libraries, in the commercial and technical library it is not only a basic ideal but one more capable of realisation than in the larger and less manageable stocks of the general libraries. Nevertheless, the cost of books only slightly revised has to be pondered; and the librarian must be on his guard against those publishers who only too often issue as a new edition a work which has only the most trivial alterations. As far as possible, new issues of text-books which do not need replacing from the purely physical point of view should be seen on approval; and when it is decided not to replace, or to replace for the commercial and technical library only, copies of the older edition should have a slip pasted on the title page warning the reader that certain passages have been altered in a newer edition otherwise unchanged, or giving such other information as is appropriate and necessary.

Discarding

Discarding is even more difficult. When librarians talk of the stock being "up-to-date" they usually mean that the most recent books and information on all subjects are available, but the statement should also imply that material which has become seriously outmoded is not in the library. It is much more difficult to discard books than to add them, but discarding is a serious problem which must be faced. Arbitrary decisions based on dates and other factors which may seem to offer incontrovertible arguments in favour of discarding may in some cases easily result in the destruction of basic material of historical value. The issue can be evaded for a time by keeping the open shelves current and relegating doubtful books to the stack, but the ever expanding catalogue will ultimately compel action. The librarian is unable to get any help from bibliographies, and if he very properly questions his own judgment in some cases, he should certainly seek expert advice. It is to be hoped that a time will come when bibliographers show as much concern with books that may do harm by being retained in a library as they now exercise in listing those they presume will do good. An authoritative "discarding" body is becoming an urgent need in days when scientific and technical developments are proceeding at a breathless pace and readers more and more expect to be given suitable books rather than exercise their own judgment in selecting them. Meanwhile, librarians who are fortunate enough to secure the services of a reliable expert in dealing with a whole class, would help their colleagues by circulating copies of his recommendations, as was done by one librarian who published a comprehensive list of additions and discards on accountancy, a subject much changed by the 1948 Companies Act.

Periodicals

The choice of periodicals is even more dependent on local needs than the selection of books, for though, in the main, the same range of interests has to be covered, the number which can be provided out of the many thousands available is so small that selection is a matter of some difficulty. On the other hand, errors are not so costly; it is easy to test their value by use and equally simple to replace them by others if they fail the test.

Every library should have the standard journals

of the professions represented in the book stock if there are sufficient practitioners in the town to justify their provision, e.g. the various branches of accountancy, medicine, etc. Some magazines of recognised importance—*Economist, Nature, Statist*—should also be taken. The bulk of the holdings will consist of trade and scientific and technical journals.

Many long established and authoritative ones will be known to the librarian—in fact, they will probably be stocked before the special library is formed—and others can be chosen from such sources as Willing's *Press Guide*, the *World List of Scientific Periodicals*, Ulrich's *Periodical Directory*, and *List of Holdings of Scientific and Technical Periodicals*, published by the Department of Scientific and Industrial Research. It is always advisable to see one or more copies before making a decision. When his choice moves into highly specialised fields, the librarian should seek advice from research workers and such learned bodies as are accessible to him, particularly in selecting journals in foreign languages.

The periodical holdings are rarely static because, now that publishing them has become a rather hazardous business, many die and new ones constantly appear. They should be regularly checked to ensure that the selection does not lag behind events such as the founding of new industries or the success of an invention, both of which usually stimulate the production of new journals. Even long established ones need attention, for their quality fluctuates mysteriously, probably reflecting

BOOK STOCK

editorial changes. Though the possession of a long file may make the librarian reluctant to change, he must not hesitate to replace any which have ceased to have relevance to current needs. When showing signs of journalistic decrepitude, they should be taken off the public racks for a time to test readers' reactions before they are discontinued.

The department should not be allowed to become a dumping place for unworthy publications given away by some publishers and propagandist organisations. A rigid check on the quality of gifts should be maintained. Different standards would, of course, apply to the magazines issued by banks and chambers of commerce, or local works journals and those of well-known firms which have acquired a reputation for the excellence of their technical articles, such as *Progress* (the magazine of Unilever).

Newspapers

The only newspapers the commercial library will generally stock are those concerned wholly with finance and shipping and certain trade and industrial supplements of the more important newspapers. The *Financial Times* and the *Stock Exchange Daily Official List* (London) should find a place, together with any local stock exchange publication. One of the largest and most successful commercial libraries in a city with extensive American connections provides the *New York Commercial and Financial Chronicle* and the *Toronto Financial Post*. This library also displays the commercial, financial, ship-

COMMERCIAL AND TECHNICAL LIBRARIES

ping and advertisement pages of *The Times, Manchester Guardian* and *Liverpool Post.* Seaport towns must have *Lloyd's List and Shipping Gazette* and may also find the *Journal of Commerce* (Liverpool) helpful.

CHAPTER VI

PATENTS AND TRADE MARKS

PATENTS

UNITED KINGDOM patent specifications and abridgments, and the name and subject indexes and other records, are supplied as published by the Patent Office to the public libraries of Belfast, Birmingham, Bolton, Bradford, Bristol, Cardiff, Glasgow, Halifax, Huddersfield, Hull, Keighley, Leeds, Leicester, Liverpool, Manchester, Newcastle-upon-Tyne (kept for the last sixteen years only), Nottingham, Preston and Sheffield. London is served by the Patent Office Library and the Science Museum Library, and Edinburgh by the Royal Scottish Museum. The annual output of specifications is about 20,000.

United States patent specifications, which reach a total of some 40,000 a year, are provided by the Patent Office at the public libraries of certain industrial centres as well as at the Patent 'Office Library itself. Some libraries also stock the patent publications of other foreign countries, but the United States issues are by far the most important to British industry. A list of the holdings of foreign patent records is given at pages 182–188.

Industrialists must have ready access to patent

COMMERCIAL AND TECHNICAL LIBRARIES

specifications relating to their own interests and to parallel lines of invention. Some of the larger firms build up their own collections and employ special staff to deal with them; others rely on Chartered Patent Agents to select and supply specifications and to notify them of developments likely to be of interest. In any case, however, the deposit public libraries are frequently called into service even by firms with excellent patents departments of their own, and smaller businesses use them extensively.

In some deposit libraries the patent library is a separate unit, but the majority find it possible to deal with enquiries through the commercial and technical library. Before the war, when the publications of the Patent Office were up to date, it was comparatively easy for an intelligent assistant to help readers to use them. Unfortunately, staffing and printing difficulties in the Patent Office during the war years and since have left gaps in the issues of abridgments and indexes, and as the classification has also been frequently adjusted to include new subjects, the task of searching is now one of considerable complexity. It is advisable, therefore, to detail two assistants whose duties overlap to study and master the procedure of search so that an adequate public service can be given.

During the past decade, the use of the patents collections has decreased in many of the deposit libraries. There are two main reasons for it. Because of the war-time deficiencies in the issue of patent publications, it is almost impossible to make a conclusive search in provincial libraries alone, and many firms which formerly relied on their own staffs to keep abreast of patent literature through them have been compelled to employ agents who can use the detailed records of the Patent Office Library. Secondly, the free-lance inventors who formerly made their own searches in public libraries are not now so numerous. Many patents are the products of systematised research and experiment in the laboratories and workshops of the large industrial combines, and the processes which ultimately lead to their acceptance are carried out by patent agents or the London staffs of the firms concerned.

A detailed statement of the present patent position can hardly be given here, but the following summary may be helpful. The reader is referred to three informative papers in ASLIB *Proceedings:* Bennett, E. M. *Searching classified Patent Specifications* (Vol. 4, pp. 75–82); Davison, G. H. *Facts concerning Patents of particular interest to Industrial Librarians and Information Officers* (Vol. 5, pp. 101–120); and Mathys, H. R. *Patents as a source of Information* (Vol. 4, pp. 69–74).

The *Official Journal (patents)*, published weekly, gives current information on applications, amendments, complete specifications accepted and patents sealed and kept in force by payment of annual fees. It also includes a subject matter index of the complete specifications listed in the issue and a group allotment index of abridgments shortly to be

COMMERCIAL AND TECHNICAL LIBRARIES

published, as well as other information on patents and registered designs. A *Group Allotment Index* is published for each series of 20,000 numbers. Another regular yearly publication is the *List of Patents in Force*.

An annual *Index to Names of Applicants in connection with Complete Specifications* was issued up to 1930, after which date each volume covers a group of 20,000 numbers. The last volume, dated 1952, includes specifications 540,001–560,000, which were published in 1944. A search in a deposit library by name of patentee involves the use of the annual index, followed by a tedious and time wasting examination of the lists in the weekly *Official Journal*, but for those who are able to visit the Patent Office Library a series of annual name indexes of applicants is maintained on cards for the current years. There are also card indexes of accepted patents under the name of the patentee for the period not covered by printed name indexes.

The *Abridgments* are abstracts of specifications and are intended to provide an easy way for searchers to examine numbers of patents without the labour of reading through the full and sometimes long and detailed specifications. After 1931 (specification No. 340,001) they were issued in 40 subject groups, and in 1949 (specification No. 600,001) the number increased to 44. This system of grouping is designed to enable those interested in particular subjects to confine their studies to them and to related subjects; by purchasing the relevant group volumes, they have at hand a convenient briefer record of all patents they may require. The abridgments are complete to specification 500,000, issued in 1939. Publication ceased at the outbreak of war, and began again at 560,001 when hostilities ceased. Since then, numbers 500,001 to 520,000 have been issued, and the first sheets of the remaining gaps have begun to appear at the time of writing. Current abridgments are in sections for binding and an index is also supplied, after some delay, when a volume is complete. There is always a time lag between the publication of the specifications and the abridgments.

The majority of enquiries received are for patents dealing with particular subjects. In trying to satisfy them the librarian will find it necessary to study with care the various indexes which have been issued from time to time. It is of course obvious that an expanding notation had to be devised to provide a symbol for each specific subject, precisely as is done in the various editions of a library classification to keep pace with the growth of knowledge, but the searcher struggling through the many changes and adaptations which have been found necessary may perhaps be forgiven for wishing that it had been possible to devise at the outset a scheme flexible enough to allow consistency of treatment. It is probable that the staff of the Patent Office, faced with an expanding range of subjects of invention which must be fitted into a limited framework designed for a simpler age, share that view.

COMMERCIAL AND TECHNICAL LIBRARIES

As the use of the subject indexes is explained in detail in Mr. Bennett's article referred to above, it is not necessary to attempt to give a full description of the processes of subject search here. It is sufficient to point out that under the present system a symbol, comprising a class number and a press mark, is provided for each specific subject. The classification symbol for the subject required can be found by using the various printed indexes, but as these cover a considerable period, during which several changes were made in the classification, it is not sufficient to find a reference in one of them; all those issued over the period of search must be examined before the searcher can be certain that he has found the correct symbol. The next step is to examine the appropriate group abridgment volumes, each of which is indexed, to find details of the actual specifications required. In searching for specifications for which the abridgments have not yet appeared, the enquirer can use either the manuscript subject indexes in the Patent Office Library, or the microfilm of them now held by many deposit libraries. The Patent Office Library is now bridging the gap between the publication of the full specification and the inclusion of the corresponding abridgment in its group by providing a classified set of full specifications, using the class marks printed on the specification and providing additional copies, where necessary, to cover more than one class.

Other publications available at the deposit libraries

PATENTS AND TRADE MARKS

are the *Annual Report of the Comptroller-General,* and the *Reports of Patent, Design, Trade Mark and other cases.* This is published monthly, and there is an annual index of cases which also contains digests of them. The librarian should have on stock for distribution to readers copies of the following pamphlets: *Instructions to Applicants for Patents; Instructions as to the preparation of Specification Drawings;* and *Instructions to persons who wish to register Designs;* all of which can be obtained on request from the Patent Office.

Photo-copying of foreign and out of print United Kingdom specifications is done at reasonable prices at the Patent Office which is well equipped to carry out this work on an extensive scale.

The unsatisfactory position in which the provincial patent searcher now finds himself has recently received most careful consideration at the Patent Office. A welcome rigidity in the subject indexing has been introduced by printing the class number and press mark on each published specification. It has now been decided to simplify the procedure of search by adopting the Powers-Samas punched card method, which has been successfully used in the United States Patent Office. Under this system, which will operate from the 1st February, 1954, in Classes 40 (7) Radio navigation, radio location and radio aerials and 40 (8) Electric impedance networks, the searcher must select the classification marks of the specifications he requires from the current Classification Key. At a charge of 10s 6d per classification mark, a File List of numbers of all specifications covered by it for the last 50 years and current to within a week of the date of the searcher's application will be supplied. Having obtained the numbers, he can then consult the specifications either at the Patent Office Library or at the nearest deposit library. To minimise the enormous wear and tear on the millions of cards by frequent sorting of them by mechanical speed processes, sorting will be carried out in subject groups.

The adoption of this system will be greeted with relief by the librarians of the deposit libraries. When it is fully in operation some time hence (for the preparation of the cards is obviously a job of some magnitude) the libraries' staffs will be relieved of the laborious and often frustrating task of helping searchers. It is possible, too, that an increased use of the patent collections will result without added strain on those who administer them.

Methods of filing patent records vary. In some libraries, the specifications are bound in volumes. Though this has the undoubted advantage of reducing the risk of misplacement, a reader consulting a large number of specifications has to handle many heavy, bound volumes, a disability shared by the staff, who must replace as well as produce them. Moreover, with costs at their present level, the annual charge for binding 20,000 specifications is considerable. In other libraries, the specifications are filed loose in boxes, into which they should be packed fairly tightly to prevent sagging. Perhaps the most convenient method is to use board folders with a cloth spine and with the ends secured by tapes to prevent the contents from slipping out of the folder. A suitable size of folder is one that will carry about 100 specifications. In the loose filing methods, only the actual specifications need be brought to the reader, but the utmost care must be taken in replacing them, for a misplaced specification is a lost one among the great number in stock. It will probably be found necessary to bind all the other United Kingdom patent publications in libraries where they are well used.

A similar method can be used for the United States specifications, whose numbers provide a serious problem for the librarian with limited stack accommodation. The recent issues are most commonly used, and if the earlier ones are rarely or never asked for, the librarian may deem it desirable to discard them when necessary. They are indexed under name and subject in the *Index of Patents issued from the United States Patent Office*, which is published weekly and reissued in annual volumes. Other foreign specifications, apart from the German, are generally so little used that there appears to be no sound reason why deposit libraries should duplicate collections already in existence, provided that the friendly collaboration which is so marked a feature of modern librarianship is extended to the interchange of foreign patent publications. Moreover, it is reasonable to suggest that the few readers who have need to inspect this material should do so at the Patent Office Library, where by far the most extensive range of foreign patent publications is on stock. It is, of course, a rule that United Kingdom patent specifications must always be available in the deposit libraries and their loan is therefore not possible.

Many journals regularly print abstracts of selected United Kingdom and foreign patents; *Chemical Abstracts* (published by the American Chemical Society) and *British Abstracts* (now superseded by separate series on much the same lines) are well-known examples. Though of little use to patent searchers, they provide a quick and easy way of keeping a check on patents relating to subjects of research, and are helpful in the preparation of scientific and technical bibliographies. Firms which check patents as published will be helped by *Patents Abstracts Journal*, now being produced by the Technical Information Company of Liverpool. The journal provides a remarkably quick and efficient service by printing abstracts of all British patents recently published, and is divided into three groups—General and Mechanical; Chemical; and Electrical.

Holdings of Commonwealth and Foreign Patents Publications in libraries in the United Kingdom

PATENT OFFICE LIBRARY

Patent specifications
These are received from the following countries:—

PATENTS AND TRADE MARKS

Australia, Austria, Belgium (full specifications since 1949 only), Bermuda, Canada (full specifications since 1949 only), Czechoslovakia (now irregularly), Denmark, Eire, Finland, France, Germany, Hungary, India, Italy, Netherlands, Norway, Poland, Sweden, Switzerland, Trinidad, United States.

There are certain gaps in the above collections owing to the war, but in the main they are very representative.

Abridgments
  Official Journals containing abridgments:—

Australia	The Australian Official Journal of Patents, Trade Marks and Designs
Belgium	Recueil des Brevets d'Invention
Canada	The Canadian Patent Office Record
Eire	Official Journal of Commercial and Industrial Property
Finland	Suomen Patentilehti
Germany	Das Patentblatt (Abridgments to 1945 only)
India	Abridgments of Specifications
Japan	Patent Gazette
Mexico	Gaceta de la Propiedad Industrial
New Zealand	Patent Office Journal
Norway	Norsk Tidende for det Industrielle Rettsvern
Poland	Wiadmosci Patentowego
Spain	Boletin Official de la Propiedad Industrial
Sweden	Svensk Tidskrift för Industriellt Rattskydd
U.S.S.R.	Bulletin of the State Bureau for the Registration of Inventions (To No. 12 of 1949 only)
U.S.A.	Official Gazette of the U.S. Patent Office

COMMERCIAL AND TECHNICAL LIBRARIES

PUBLIC LIBRARIES

AUSTRALIA

Patent specifications
Birmingham, Glasgow and Manchester, 1904 to date.
Official Journal of Patents (containing abridgments)
Birmingham, 1905 to date; Glasgow, 1907 to date; Manchester, 1904 to date.

QUEENSLAND

Patents (abridgments)
Manchester, 1860 to 1885.

VICTORIA

Patent specifications
Manchester, 1854 to 1888.
Patents and Patentees. Indexes (containing abridgments)
Manchester, 1873 to 1891.

WESTERN AUSTRALIA

Supplement to Government Gazette (containing lists of complete specifications accepted, etc.)
Manchester, 1899 to 1906.

CANADA

Patent Office Record (containing abridgments)
Belfast, 1943 to date; Birmingham, 1873 to date; Bolton, 1931 to date; Bristol, 1938 to date; Glasgow, 1879 to date; Hull, 1940 to date; Leeds, 1928 to date; Manchester, 1873 to date; Nottingham, 1947 to date; Sheffield, 1950 to date.
Patents of Canada
Manchester, one volume containing brief descriptions of specifications from 1824 to 1849.

PATENTS AND TRADE MARKS

EIRE

Patent specifications
 Belfast, Birmingham, Glasgow and Manchester, 1927-8 to date.
Official Journal of Industrial and Commercial Property (containing abridgments and Trade Marks)
 Belfast, Birmingham, Glasgow and Manchester, 1928 to date.

GERMANY

Leeds holds the following:—
 Patentschriften
  Pre-war specifications 80974 (1896)—678,143 (August, 1939).
  War time specifications. On request the Patent Office has agreed to furnish Leeds free of charge with photo-copies of any German War-time specifications held in London. In addition to this a number of these War-time specifications, publication of which had been delayed, are now being issued each week by the German Patent Office. They are in the range 680,000 to 767,000 and in September, 1953 totalled some 5,000.
  Post-war specifications 800,001 onwards.

 Indexes
  The following four items are general indexes not confined to any one year:—
  Nummernliste der deutschen Patentschriften mit Angabe der Klasse, Unterklasse und Gruppe. 1934. (Numerical list of patents giving allocations into classes, sub-classes and groups, from Specification No. 1 to 567, 340, December, 1932. A similar

weekly list has been received with the first post-war specifications.)

Gruppenliste der deutschen Patentschriften mit Angabe der zu jeder Klasse, Unterklasse, und Gruppe gehörenden Nummern. 1934.
(List of specifications arranged under classes and groups, from Specification No. 1 to 567,340, December, 1932.)

Later editions of the above two indexes have been published, but were out of print when the delivery of German specifications began again in 1953.

Stichwörterverzeichnis. Alphabetische Zusammenstellung technischer Gegenstände mit Angabe der dazugehörigen Patentklassen, Gruppen und Untergruppen. 1951.
(Subject index to the patent classification.)

Gruppeneinteilung der Patentklassen. 1949.
(List of patent classes and groups.)

Annual Index.

Verzeichnis der vom erteilten Patente...	Reichspatentamt im Jahre [1937] 1896–1937, 1940, 1942, and to date, as published.
Abschnitt 1(a)	Nach den Nummern geordnete Ubersicht... (Numerical list giving allocation to classes, etc., also acceptance and issuing dates.)
(b)	Nach den Aktenzeichen geordnete Ubersicht... (Numerical list arranged under "application, or provisional, numbers" and giving allocations to classes, etc. and final patent num-

PATENTS AND TRADE MARKS

      bers. This "Part B" first appeared in the annual index for 1926.)
2. Nach Patentklassen geordnete Ubersicht...
   (List of patents arranged by classes.)
3. Namenverzeichnis der Patentinhaber.
   (Index of patentees.)
4. Verzeichnis der in die Patentrolle eingetragenen und am 1 März [1938] noch nicht gelöschten Patente.
   (List of patents in force.)

      Sections 1(a) and 2 of these annual indexes supplement the first two of the general indexes, the Nummernliste and the Gruppenliste mentioned above.

Patentblatt und Auszüge aus den Patentschriften
    Glasgow, 1926 to 1939; Leeds, 1950 to date.

NEW ZEALAND

Patent Office Journal (containing abridgments)
    Birmingham, 1912 to date; Glasgow, 1914 to 1939; Manchester, 1914 to date.

SOUTH AFRICA

Official Journal of Patents, Trade Marks, Designs and Copyright
    Manchester, 1948 to date.

COMMERCIAL AND TECHNICAL LIBRARIES

UNITED STATES

Patent specifications
   Birmingham, last 50 years; Glasgow, Leeds, and Manchester, 1893 to date; Sheffield, last 17 years.

Plant specifications
   Birmingham, Glasgow, Leeds, Manchester and Sheffield, 1931 to date.

Index of Patents issued from the United States Patent Office
   Files for varying periods are held by the above libraries.

Annual Report of the Commissioner of Patents
   Manchester, 1865 to 1871, 1876 to 1919.

Official Gazette (containing abridgments)
   Birmingham, 1872 to date; Glasgow, 1929 to 1951; Leeds, 1872 to date; Manchester, 1880 to date.

General Index of the Official Gazette and monthly volumes of Patents of the United States Patent Office
   Manchester, 1872 to 1875.

Liverpool has holdings of patent publications of Australia, Canada, Eire, New Zealand and the United States, but many of the files were destroyed by enemy action and have not yet been completely replaced.

TRADE MARKS

A Trade Mark is a distinctive symbol—a word, usually a fanciful or invented one, or a design, or a combination of both—used by a manufacturer or trader in relation to his goods for the purpose of distinguishing them from the similar goods of other manufacturers or traders. The act of registration of a trade mark entitles the owner of the mark to bring an action for infringement against anyone using the same or a similar mark in relation to the same goods. Application for registration should be made to the Registrar at the Patent Office. Alternatively, in the case of textile marks, applications may be sent to the Manchester Branch of the Trade Marks Registry; or, in the case of marks for metal goods, to the Cutlers' Company, Sheffield, if the applicant is carrying on business in Hallamshire or within six miles thereof. Registration lasts for seven years, and can be renewed for further periods of fourteen years by payment of the requisite fee. A pamphlet entitled *Instructions to persons who wish to register Trade Marks* is issued by the Patent Office for free distribution to intending applicants. It describes, clearly and briefly, the whole procedure of application for and registration of trade marks, and librarians should keep a small stock for the use of intending applicants.

An accepted mark is advertised in the *Trade Marks Journal*, first published in 1876 and issued weekly to all patent deposit libraries. It has an index of names of applicants.

The help the commercial and technical librarian can give to an intending applicant for the registration of a trade mark is somewhat limited. He should, of course, give him a copy of the above mentioned pamphlet, and show him the two following Patent Office publications, from which he can find out how many application forms he must submit: *List of Goods in each of the classes of the Substituted Classification of Goods* and *Alphabetical Index to the Substituted Classification of Goods*, both published in 1938 in connection with the Trade Marks Act of that year. The enquirer may also find it useful to see examples of already advertised marks in the *Trade Marks Journal*.

It is obviously impossible for the Patent Office to print an index of registered marks on the detailed lines of those published for patents. On application, the Registrar will cause a check to be made whether a mark submitted is on record. If the enquirer wishes, he may himself undertake a search among the classified representations and indexes of trade marks in the Patent Office. Similar searches can also be made for marks for textile goods at Manchester. All these searches are made subject to a fee.

The usual library enquiry is "What firm uses a certain trade mark?" Several sources help the librarian to answer this question. Some directories provide alphabetical lists of trade names, and these are probably the most useful; lists of marks are also given in certain journals, such as *Paint, Oil and Colour Journal; Food Processing, Packaging and Marketing; Men's Wear*, etc. These are particularly valuable for tracing recently published marks. In addition, certain journals publish annual supplements or year books, which include lists of trade marks and names —for example: *Decorator Trade Reference Book and Diary; Cabinet Maker Year Book and Buyers' Guide;*

PATENTS AND TRADE MARKS

Ironmonger Directory of Branded Hardware; Machinery Market Year Book, etc. Sometimes periodicals publish full lists running through several issues. *Iron Age* (American) published 10,000 trade names, an alphabetical list spread over six months' weekly parts; *Chemical Engineering* (American) publishes a list in the December copy each year; and *Welding* issued a special list of trade names for welding equipment in the September, 1949 number. Other useful sources are published by the National Trade Press and Heywood's, such as *Footwear: Directory of Trade Marks and Trade Names; Watchmaker, Jeweller and Silversmith: Directory of Trade Names and Punch Marks; Furnishing Show Book and Directory of Trade Names; and Fashions and Fabrics: Branded Merchandise and Trade Marks Directory*. Another new publication, which will probably increase in value as the number of subscribers grows, is the *Directory* issued by the Trade Marks Directory Service.

It is advisable to record in the directory index the fact that a directory includes a list of trade marks. If many enquiries are received, it may be considered worth while to compile a card index of marks listed in other publications which are not so well known as sources of information. As in other indexes made by the librarian, the labour involved in its compilation should be measured against the time taken to satisfy enquirers without it.

CHAPTER VII

ORGANISATION AND ADMINISTRATION

MANY of the administrative methods of the commercial and technical library, particularly those affecting the public service, must conform in the main to the general organisation of the composite library system of which it is a part. Other services are peculiar to the department and are dealt with in some detail in this chapter, but some of the general methods also justify special treatment.

Reference or joint reference and home reading library

If the building is suitable the question may arise whether the American practice of making it a joint reference and home reading library should be followed.

At first sight there appear to be certain advantages in adopting such a course. The librarian's experience in administering a library comprising comparatively few subjects, which makes his book selection and his advisory service to readers highly competent, could be offered to a much larger public; home reading borrowers would see wider ranges of books and periodicals; and the concentration of the stock in one department would increase their

ORGANISATION AND ADMINISTRATION

chances of obtaining the books they want. Though expenditure on books would increase at first because much duplication would be necessary, in later years it would probably be less than before the union.

The librarian contemplating this step would have to decide whether to transfer from the lending library *all* the books on the subjects covered or only those of advanced standard. In the former case, the increased use of the library by "popular" readers—whose heaviest borrowings would coincide with the influx of readers of periodicals on Fridays and Saturdays (when most journals appear)—might well make serious study impossible. If only advanced books were stocked, and the more elementary books still remained in the lending library, readers in both departments would be inconvenienced, since the advanced reader sometimes wishes to clarify a point in a less erudite work and vice versa.

In a joint library books must be divided into "no-loan" and home reading—for a basic stock of purely reference and standard books must always be at hand—and arguments will inevitably arise when disappointed borrowers demand to know why all of them cannot be lent. Some users of the science and technology library are becoming more and more unwilling to work in a library, and many are quite ready to complain that the only time they can study even such books as Thorpe's *Dictionary of Applied Chemistry* or Kempe's *Engineers' Year Book* is in the evenings by their own firesides. Though such readers have an undoubted nuisance value,

COMMERCIAL AND TECHNICAL LIBRARIES

their complaints in a large new technical library where only advanced books are provided are not considered to be serious enough to call into question the wisdom of using the library for both purposes.

The librarian's decision will also depend on the way the library has developed. If it has hitherto provided a normal reference service and has few active industrial and research connections, the change might well be successful. If, on the other hand, it is already an extremely busy library with a firm place in the city's business and industrial life, dealing each year with thousands of enquiries and undertaking searches for research purposes, the advent of a home reading public would react unfavourably on its work. Some of the staff's time, now devoted to special work with readers, would be diverted to the mechanics of issue.

The fact that American libraries run such joint libraries successfully is not wholly relevant. The comparative use of public libraries is much less there than in Britain; their readers are used to departmental libraries; and their more generous finances allow them to provide books on a scale beyond the reach of all but the most prosperous public libraries in this country.

If a joint reference and home reading library is established, it may become necessary, in certain circumstances, to provide a students' room for advanced work, with easy access to the books and periodicals.

ORGANISATION AND ADMINISTRATION

Degree of independence

One of the earliest administrative decisions which will have to be made is the amount of independence to be allowed to the librarian. The selection of books and periodicals is highly specialised; the staff's contacts with the public by correspondence and by telephone are generally more numerous and urgent than in other departments; and the nature of the service involves frequent changes in organisation. The librarian may claim with some justice that no one but he is fully conversant with readers' needs and that interference with his work may be unjustified and unhelpful. On the other hand, the chief librarian must have means of satisfying himself that the department is working properly, even though its librarian is known to be competent and industrious. The reconciliation of these points of view is a matter of some judgment and delicacy, for much depends on the right decision being made.

To some extent the final choice must be affected by the general organisation in operation throughout the system and the amount of departmental freedom it allows. For example, the chief librarian must keep a check on expenditure on books even when there is a fixed allocation of funds to the different libraries. Moreover, he must try to prevent the growth of excessive departmentalism, and the jealousies, misunderstandings and deliberate obstruction which sometimes arise from it, by ensuring that a too enthusiastic librarian does not encroach on his colleagues' work by extending his book stock into subjects allotted to them. All new book purchases should therefore be subject to central approval, but the chief will be well advised if he interferes only rarely with the librarian's recommendations and then with very good cause. Discarding and replacement should be left to him within a framework of agreed principles.

Once the basic methods have been laid down, the commercial and technical librarian should be given a reasonably free hand in general administration provided that he submits to higher authority proposed changes affecting systems in common use. The techniques of public service should not differ in the various branches of the reference library; classification and cataloguing, for example, should be closely co-ordinated. Beyond this, experiments in detailed methods should be encouraged. It may sometimes lead to irritating reversals of administrative detail when several librarians successively hold the post, but the chief librarian should bear with patience the natural desire of each to prove how much better his ideas are than those of his predecessors.

Personal contacts play so large a part in successful administration that the librarian and his staff should be helped in every way to make and maintain them. It is a good plan to arrange for a new librarian to visit the consuls and other officials of foreign governments and the more important firms where he can make the acquaintance of their librarians, information officers and research workers. The chief librarian should never interpose himself between the staff and readers; indeed, wherever possible he should add to the librarian's prestige by inviting him to make decisions in the course of his contacts with important users of the library without invoking higher authority. A petty minded chief officer, jealous of his own prerogatives, can be a very severe handicap to an enterprising commercial and technical librarian; a wise and competent chief will allow him as much freedom as possible and judge his work by results.

Correspondence

There is much to be said for giving the librarian authority to correspond directly with his clients on departmental notepaper carrying his name. In a large library system the chief librarian must work on the general principle of departmental responsibility and allow the bulk of the correspondence to go direct to and from the various libraries, merely reserving to himself the right to sign personally letters of particular significance or importance; and this can only be done by making the heads responsible for deciding which outgoing letters to submit to him. On the other hand, incoming correspondence provides the chief librarian with one of his few simple and regular means of keeping in touch with the work of the system. He will not be interested in purely repetitive routine letters, but he may find it profitable to arrange for copies of non-routine outgoing correspondence not signed by him to be submitted the following day, so that he can keep himself current with the department's main activities and be able to deal more or less adequately with those telephone enquirers who mistakenly assume that he has the details of every branch of the service at his finger tips.

There is unlikely to be sufficient departmental correspondence to justify the appointment of a secretarial assistant, though it is not unknown for the librarian, in the course of his empire building, to ask for one. Like his senior colleagues, he will be able to call on the staff of the secretarial and typing pool for dictation. A good deal of copy typing is required, but the smaller jobs can usually be done by the staff themselves. A library assistant should be expected to be able to perform creditably on the typewriter; it is often uneconomic to write copy which later must be typed.

All correspondence should be filed with the general library correspondence, where it can be uniformly classed and indexed by the filing assistant.

None of these considerations applies to the separate commercial library in the business quarter, which must be largely self-contained in these matters.

Staff training and routine

The commercial and technical library must have a staff fully competent in library technique, and able and willing to give a high standard of personal

ORGANISATION AND ADMINISTRATION

service. They must be supported by an organisation which has been carefully and intelligently planned to serve two purposes: to make it easy for the reader to obtain the information he wants, and to provide a framework of method by means of which the staff can carry out their duties efficiently, and add to their personal and professional competence while doing so.

This last point is important. It has already been stressed in chapter four and some practical suggestions are added here. Few people in any walk of life are naturally endowed with the habits of mind and action needed for the successful administration of an institution so much concerned with minutiæ as a library. They must be trained to acquire them, and the only way to do this is to plan the organisation so that they are developed by practice, and encouraged by supervision. Work requiring accuracy and observation should be checked either by examining sections of the work done or by evolving systems in routine processes by means of which the assistant can prove his own results. In certain duties carried out by more than one assistant as, for example, the receipt of current periodicals, the records should carry the initials or mark of the person checking the entry so that those who make mistakes can be identified; for the same reason other work should be allotted as a fixed duty to certain assistants. Systems of basic check, such as reverting to the original record in processes of repetitive copying, will reduce the possibility of error. There are many other ways of ensuring that assistants—except the small number who can never be taught these things and will always be incompetent librarians—reach high standards of efficiency in even the dreariest routine methods.

Some librarians may feel that the importance of accuracy in the performance of regular duties in a research and information library can be overstressed. They may repeat the common argument that bibliographical excellence is all that really matters: provide the right material and knowledgeable service, they say, and the library will be successful. These are, of course, of fundamental importance, but there is no reason why the administrative processes should not be equally well done, for the good librarian should show competence in all his work. A library service cannot be effective if two different scales of values are applied to its administration. Even in a special library, the reader is usually better able to judge the practical aspects of the service than the purely professional ones. The dreamiest of scholars expects, and has a right to expect, to receive the actual books he asks for in good condition and without an unreasonably long wait, and both he and the commercial and technical user will resent inattention and slovenly service. The department's work should therefore be as efficient as forethought, staff training and well-planned organisation can make it. Operational ineptitude in a library containing books extolling the virtues of business efficiency is hardly likely to arouse the respect of those who use it.

ORGANISATION AND ADMINISTRATION

Public service

In addition to efficiency in routine, the staff must be trained to give competent and courteous service, for on this vital point of contact all else depends. Nothing is more indicative of the standards of a library, or more appreciated by readers when given, than speed, accuracy and general competence at the counter. The staff should be discouraged from dividing themselves into counter assistants and back-room workers; all should clearly understand that the public service has undisputed priority over all other work. The service point should never be left unattended, for a library does not deserve the name unless a visible librarian is in charge of it and instantly available for consultation. At slack periods it may be possible and administratively advantageous to have only one or two assistants at the service point, where frequent interruptions make work requiring continuous application difficult. As one assistant cannot deal with several readers at once—though a particularly quick and able worker can usually contrive to satisfy a number of simple enquiries while engaged on a more difficult one—an electric buzzer should connect the counter with the workroom so that the service assistants can obtain help when several readers require attention. The next workroom assistant detailed on the rota for service should immediately drop any work on which he is engaged and go to the assistance of his colleagues; and if the need is pressing, another should be called out.

COMMERCIAL AND TECHNICAL LIBRARIES

Though the public service must have priority over other tasks, a sensible balance of values must be reached between them. Except perhaps at peak periods, it would be absurd to engage all the staff on it at one time; they would not be needed and other duties requiring concentrated effort would be neglected or badly done. Moreover, readers seeing several assistants on duty together may get the impression that the library is overstaffed, as they have little understanding of the amount of detailed work required. This would inevitably arouse criticism from a ratepaying public usually willing to give credence to the stories of municipal extravagance that so delight the popular press. Local criticism is a force to be reckoned with and the public can find plenty of grounds for adverse criticism of municipal officers without the librarian offering others to them. Only the essential minimum of staff should be on view; the others should work in the workroom; but the rules about instantly answering a service call should be rigidly enforced. Assistants should be asked not to bunch together in public when discussing the department's problems; the proper place for such conferences is the workroom.

It will be seen that the staff are expected to aim at high standards of service, but they are not likely to reach them unless the librarian provides the right kind of leadership. The hard discipline of strictly applied method is usually only willingly accepted if it is justly shared by all; younger assistants rarely bring keenness to their work unless their seniors show ability and application. The librarian and senior staff must take a fair share of difficult duty times, be prepared to do any job themselves, accept responsibility for bad work instead of blaming their juniors to the public or chief librarian, and protect their younger colleagues from the occasional rudeness of a few ill-mannered readers. A conscientious, just, able and hardworking librarian can get his staff to perform miracles of productive effort and arouse a remarkable departmental *esprit de corps*. He will be wise if he accepts for himself more onerous duties than he asks his assistants to undertake, for if he does so, they have no grounds for complaint about any methods or conditions they may be asked to follow. Whatever the pressure of other duties, he should make a regular practice of taking spells of counter duty to keep in touch with the library's users and their needs.

Hours of opening

Opening times should be based on a reasonable compromise between the needs of readers and the staff. There is no point in keeping open a commercial information service library in the business quarter when the insurance, banking, shipping and other commercial houses are closed. In a joint library in the central building, where many readers study in the evenings and on Saturdays, general reference library hours are advisable, but directories should be available at 9 a.m. for use by commercial representatives.

COMMERCIAL AND TECHNICAL LIBRARIES

Control of stock

In the case of a joint department administered as a reference library, every book recorded in the catalogue should be reasonably available at any time. The importance of this simple principle is often underestimated. Two considerations are involved: whether books are never to be lent out in any circumstances, and what methods are adopted to check misplacement and theft.

If a strict "no-loan" rule is applied, the library cannot take part in any inter-library exchange schemes, and as most libraries receive through them at least as much as they lend it would hardly be sensible to adopt such a rule. On the few occasions when a reader requires a book which has been lent in this way any indignation he may feel can usually be dispelled by an explanation of the position. These considerations apply with equal force to a local interchange scheme with industrial organisations, though in this case any book on loan can be quickly obtained. Apart from these two exceptions, however, "no loan" should be the rule. It is assumed that the central home reading library will have copies of most of the books stocked in the commercial and technical library except those of a purely reference or highly specialised kind.

Provided that the open shelf stock is not too large, the worst effects of misplacement can be overcome by checking its order at least once daily. As even the best assistant may become careless when engaged on this tedious yet exacting job, the

ORGANISATION AND ADMINISTRATION

senior staff should make a daily test check of one or two tiers and point out any errors. Quick reference sections, such as directories, codes, etc., should be straightened and placed in correct order many times each day.

Theft is a much more serious problem because books may be out of service for long periods until their loss is discovered. Readers cannot wholly be depended on to report missing books, and stock-taking checks should therefore be made of open shelf books as frequently as the other responsibilities of the staff allow. If the major part of the stock is on open shelves, complete stock checks can only be made occasionally. In this case it is advisable to concentrate on those sections which are important, are in constant use, and from which thefts are more common. As books are constantly being transferred from open shelves to stack and sometimes vice versa, a simple card stock record of open shelf books should be made additional to the stock register proper. Habits of automatic observation by the staff, and judicious action against suspected readers, help to reduce losses by theft.

Control of readers

While it is highly desirable to protect books from theft or damage, the librarian should not allow surveillance to become so keen that it might do harm to the library. The great majority of readers have a high sense of public responsibility, and it would be a mistake to introduce irritating routines because a few of them, mostly casuals, do not reach this standard. All general measures adopted should be unobtrusive, and the utmost freedom in the use of the library consonant with common sense should be allowed. Nevertheless, strong individual action should be taken against persons who enter the library without any intention of using its services properly. Tramps, loafers and the mentally unbalanced always gravitate to a public library and sometimes penetrate into the most strictly ordered special library; others think of it as a pleasant place where they can sit and read newspapers. Business touts who attempt to use the library as an office, and others who arrange to meet in it to discuss their affairs, are also troublesome. It is advisable to have in force a regulation empowering the librarian to "remove from the library any person not using it for the purpose for which it is intended", a wide clause under which he can deal effectively with all these undesirables.

Classification

The librarian may be tempted to adopt a detailed scheme such as the Universal Decimal Classification, as is done with advantage in many libraries of societies, professional bodies and industrial research organisations. Such libraries cover few subjects, each with a great deal of material. The stock needs close sub-division if its arrangement is to be suitable for the specialists who normally use it. A public departmental library, on the other hand, has a much wider range of subjects, including many which are only represented by more general books, and in this case a very detailed classification can in practice become a barrier between books and readers. Even in a general scheme, few books fall with ease and certainty into suitable classes, and the narrower the class, the more difficult it is to make accurate placings. There is thus a danger that the classifier's interpretation of a book's scope and its place in the classification may not coincide with that of the reader, who naturally assumes that the material carrying a particular class number on the shelves represents the library's full holdings. As there are comparatively few users of private special libraries, their staffs are able to overcome any difficulties of close classification by expert personal service. The commercial and technical librarian, whose readers are numerous and of many types, has not the same opportunities for close personal contacts, particularly on very busy days. He must therefore adopt methods which help readers to find books themselves. If the classes are wide enough to ensure, with a reasonable degree of certainty, that each book has a definite bearing on the subject represented by the class number, the reader in an open access library, who is the best judge of what he needs, can make his own choice. With a broader classification he is less likely to be led astray by any misjudgment in the classifier's interpretation of their contents.

From this point of view, a general library scheme, such as Dewey, is quite adequate. There will, of course, be a few subjects—usually connected with the basic trade or industry of the town—in which closer classification is desirable. It is quite possible to apply a local expansion to them without creating a notation which may run to an absurd length; and the weaknesses of some of the scientific and technical classes in Dewey can be strengthened with equal ease.

One overriding factor will affect the choice of a classification. If the existing reference libraries are already classified under one of the accepted systems, it is hard to suggest any sound reason for adopting another and more detailed one for the commercial and technical library. The difficulties of doing so will be increased if there is a union reference library catalogue. Moreover, the reader who had to pursue part of his studies in another department of the reference libraries would be confused by the existence of two classifications. The librarian must judge whether the additional work caused and the misunderstandings which would inevitably arise through the adoption of a classification more detailed than the normal scheme in use in other departments would be balanced by increased efficiency in other ways.

The catalogue

Should the catalogue be dictionary or classified? Here again, the form of the union reference library catalogue, if there is one, must govern that of the special department if much additional, and perhaps unnecessary, adminstrative work is to be avoided.

ORGANISATION AND ADMINISTRATION

It may be permissible at this point for the writer to state a personal preference for the dictionary catalogue, and to express regret that so many librarians have allowed themselves to be persuaded to adopt the classified form.

The labour of altering the whole of the catalogues of the large library systems which alone provide commercial and technical libraries is so great that few could attempt it; nevertheless, if there is any reasonable possibility of changing from the classified to the dictionary form, the librarian would be well advised to consider it. The simplicity of an alphabetical record to the reader, who is used to alphabetised arrangements, and the scope the dictionary catalogue offers for adequate and varied subject recording, are worthy of attention. It may be that the comparative neglect of catalogues in almost every public library is largely due to the cult of the classified catalogue which, though simple to make, is not so effective a guide to the library's contents as the dictionary, and is confusing to the reader. American librarians are wiser.

Cataloguing for the public catalogue in the commercial and technical library should generally follow accepted practice, and it is only necessary here to refer to a few special features. It is essential to note dates and editions; the entries, without being overloaded with bibliographical detail, should be complete enough to allow the reader to identify a particular edition of a book, and the contents of serial or multi-volume publications should be fully listed. When the stock is limited, the use of added and analytical entries might well be carried to considerable lengths. The library is concerned with local interests and industries; the librarian should be familiar with their requirements and should also know whether the published literature about them is strong or weak. When cataloguing new books, he should examine each one carefully to see whether in any way—perhaps in a chapter, or a series of chapters, or even, in special cases, in one vital reference—it provides new or additional information of local commercial or industrial value. If it does, the fact should be recorded on the main card and on one or more analytical entries under the appropriate subject headings. In special cases of this nature it may be thought desirable to include references to some important articles in periodicals on file.

This method of cataloguing should not be confused with the staff information or other indexes, which will be dealt with later. If space allows the public catalogue to be built up in this way, there is no reason (except staffing difficulties) why it should not be as complete a guide to the library's contents, as distinct from a record of book titles, as the librarian can make it. Matters dealt with by analyticals would not be duplicated in the staff index of information. Not every reader consults the staff, however warmly he is invited to do so, and if he confines his search to a catalogue which does not provide him with sufficient detail, he may leave the library as that most deplorable of a librarian's failures, the dissatisfied reader who thinks the library cannot give him the information he wants.

The preparation and maintenance of so detailed a catalogue would make heavy demands on the time and skill of the staff, particularly if it is in dictionary form. If there are many analytical entries (and the limit to be set can only be based on the librarian's judgment of the balance of values between the worth of the entries and the amount of work they cause), a valuable public record of information available in the library would be created. To keep its size within reasonable bounds, regular weeding of the analytical entries would be needed. New books would have to be examined, not only to find whether they provided material for further entries, but also to see whether they contained matter which cancelled out analytical entries already in the catalogue. In a small library with limited resources the expansion of the catalogue on these lines would add value to the stock; in the larger libraries it may probably be thought sufficient to provide analyticals only in certain important aspects of local industry about which there is little recorded information.

The card catalogue is undoubtedly the most flexible form yet invented, but there are many objections to it. The public do not find it easy to use; it occupies a great deal of space; and only one entry can be seen at a time. The sheaf form has certain advantages, being easier to handle and less costly in material and space, but the time taken to insert and abstract slips is a disadvantage, particularly if many analytical entries are included. Until someone invents a new kind of catalogue which will give the reader a sight of several entries at once and be easy to keep current, the librarian must do his best with the material available to him. The balance of choice generally leans towards the card form for the public catalogue; but for subsidiary records such as those used for periodicals, directories, etc., other and from the public point of view, simpler methods, may be preferred.

Stock records

In the larger libraries clerical systems are commonly standardised to simplify administration and save the cost of printing a variety of ruled books and forms. If the central book buying department's order books or loose-leaf slips serve as an accession register, it may be thought unnecessary to duplicate it in the commercial and technical library; the departmental analysis of book expenditure can be made by recording the class and cost of all books as they are prepared for service, provided that the book order department notes the price in each book processed. The trend is towards simplicity in such unified methods, perhaps because mounting costs are causing librarians to re-examine their administration to see whether economies are possible by eliminating records which either duplicate others or do not serve a really vital purpose.

As frequent checks must be made of the open

shelf books so that missing books can be noted and quickly replaced, the shelf or stock register should be accurate, current and flexible. Card systems meet these requirements, but unless the staff have reached high standards of accuracy in working them, misplaced and even lost cards can result in much confusion, and some librarians with long experience of card records dislike them for this reason. Many types of shelf register are in use, and the choice of a suitable one must be left to individual preference. If the entries are sensibly spaced to begin with, a loose-leaf shelf register allows a considerable degree of flexibility and there is no danger of misplaced entries. One method which obviates the need for two records may be worth consideration in a library with a classified catalogue. If each catalogue card in the main class sequence is suitably ruled on the back, it can be used as a stock record, and, indeed, as a complete "history" card of the particular book it represents. This system is perhaps more suitable for lending libraries, where the library life of most books is short, and where the absence of catalogue drawers during stock-taking is not so serious. Some librarians may feel that a more permanent kind of record than the elusive card is needed in a library of reference, even in the commercial and technical department, where some of the books have a reasonably long life. It is assumed, of course, that the stock will be kept current by regularly weeding out those books which have little or no claim to the kind of bibliographical immortality which the librarian trained in a general reference library likes to bestow on his collection.

Issue methods

Ideally, there should be no need to keep a record of issues, but librarians, who so often have to justify the cost of their services to critical finance committees, generally find it advisable to be able to prove statistically that the department is earning its keep. There is no difficulty in recording issues of books from the stack, since the only practical method of service is to make readers complete application forms for them from which an analysis of the day's issue can be made when the record has been cleared by the return of the book.

Open shelf books, which are most frequently used and may comprise a large part of the stock, are not so easily dealt with. Readers often fail to record the books they use even when issue slips inviting them to do so are near at hand. If readers are asked to leave their books on the tables after use, issue returns can be made from them. This is unsatisfactory because there can be no guarantee either that the books so left have been used for study or that others have not been read and replaced. It is generally assumed that these points cancel out, and that the recorded issues of open shelf books made in this way are a fair measure of the number of books used. It may be thought that regular counts of readers in the library at, say, half-hourly intervals in a business commercial library or hourly ones in a full-scale joint library, may be sufficient. One danger must be borne in mind. It is only possible to check the accuracy of issue records of books loaned from the stack on readers' application forms, and a librarian faced with a declining service may be tempted to inflate his other statistics, particularly if—as is usually the case—the standing of the department, involving such matters as the number of staff allotted to it and even their salary grades, is judged, as it reasonably can be, on the use made of the library. If this is thought to be a fanciful objection it may be stated that the writer has had experience of a systematic inflation of issues over a long period with results that for a time were a grave embarrassment to the chief librarian and the committee.

Whatever method of issue is adopted, and even if no record is kept, it is always advisable, in a library in which use must play an important part in book selection, to note in each book the number of times it has been used; all that is needed is a label inside one cover on which the date of issue can be stamped or written. Such records are useful when decisions have to be made whether further copies of individual books should be bought or whether the stock in certain classes needs strengthening; observation is not always a reliable guide.

Many items will be excluded from the issue statistics for practical reasons. It would be a needless irritation to readers to ask them to complete an issue slip every time they use a directory for the few moments such consultations usually take, and if they are invited to leave these heavily used books on the tables replacement would be a considerable job for the staff. Other quick reference material in almost constant service should also be issued without record. There is no point in attempting to compile issues of trade catalogues, or of printed periodical indexes and similar publications which merely supplement the catalogue. It may be permissible to make an estimated record of the use of directories should local conditions require justification of the high cost of their provision. Unless no statistics are kept for any books, all quick reference material the issues of which are not recorded is better shelved apart from the main sequence.

Daily, monthly and other issue returns will naturally be in line with the general methods in use in all other departments.

Periodicals

The current issue of any periodical taken must always be available; the files, whether bound or unbound, must be complete within the limits set for them; the reader must be able to find the current one he wants easily and quickly.

Every librarian tries to observe these simple conditions and finds that it is not easy to do so when large numbers of periodicals are taken. Commercial and technical libraries purchase several hundred, and also accept house journals of local firms, magazines issued by banks, chambers of commerce, etc. They are published at varying times,

ORGANISATION AND ADMINISTRATION

and foreign periodicals are subject to the vicissitudes of post, shipping and air travel. Each of them must be in the library when it is "due"—that is, when it is available for purchase at newsagents; and the library that cherishes a good reputation should never fail to provide it.

In the first place, it is advisable to set standards in the periodicals taken; a gift should not be accepted merely because it is a gift. It is a good principle to assess its value on precisely the same conditions as are applied to a purchase; if it is decided to accept it, the donor should be asked to guarantee its supply regularly and promptly for at least a year. The gift should then be treated in all respects as a bought periodical, even by sending reminders if it is overdue.

Many methods of recording the receipt of periodicals are in use, and one most suitable for the requirements of the department must be adopted. It should ensure accuracy in the check of incoming issues and immediately declare those not supplied; it should record source, period of publication, cost, date due, and date of issue of title page and index. It is helpful, too, to include details of its ultimate disposal, e.g. when a volume begins, number of parts comprising a volume and the duration of the file. No liberties can be taken with periodicals and their files in the commercial and technical library; everything should move with almost mechanical precision so that each file is correct, for periodicals are the life blood of research.

COMMERCIAL AND TECHNICAL LIBRARIES

It is by no means uncommon even today, when war shortages have been largely overcome, for periodicals to be stolen. It should not be left to readers to tell the staff that a periodical is missing; if thefts are fairly frequent the racks should be checked daily so that a new copy of any one stolen can be obtained as soon as possible. It would be wanted in any case for file. If losses are few, or confined to one or more very popular magazines, it is doubtful whether the time spent in a daily check will be justified. Regular thefts of certain periodicals can be guarded against by taking them off the public racks for a time and issuing them on request.

Whether the periodicals dealing with commerce and trade should be displayed separately from those on technical matters depends on a similar decision to be made about the arrangement of the two branches of the service in the one library. Periodicals can be arranged alphabetically by title or by subject; if the latter method is adopted, the subjects themselves must run either by the classification or alphabetically. It would be unprofitable to argue here the merits of either system, because the decision as to which to adopt depends not on set principles but on the kind of reader using the periodicals and the purposes for which he needs them. In some special libraries there are sound practical reasons for grouping by class and perhaps for shelving the current and some recent numbers with the books at that class; but the readership of the public commercial and technical library is so varied that an alphabetical arrangement by title, on special racks, will probably best serve the majority of users. Most of them ask or look for periodicals either by title or by some well-known contraction of the title. Moreover, if all periodicals are displayed without cases on open racks which allow each to be readily identified, the difficulties in alphabetisation caused by the number of periodicals carrying such common introductory words as "Journal of" or "Review of" do not trouble the reader, who easily recognises the familiar covers of those he wants.

Periodical index

An index to periodicals is an obvious need. Some librarians prefer to use one of the visible types on the market. These have many good points: the entries are easily seen; they are flexible; but if the very full type of index advocated below is adopted, a visible method containing so many entries would become very cumbrous, though the card-wheel type may be worth consideration. Others fly to the inevitable card-drawer index, which allows any number of entries, but suffers from the defects of all such records. The writer has used for many years a typewritten, foolscap size, loose-leaf index, each page containing some twelve entries with four spaces left between them for additions. This has all the advantages of the printed page; it is easy to use; and can be placed on the periodical rack itself. Its very popularity might reasonably be urged against it, because wear and tear will often make it necessary to retype certain pages long before recorded changes in the entries compel a revision. Paper of good quality and a record ribbon must be used; carbon copies are quite useless. The actual amount of retyping needed is not large, and if the revision of small sections is undertaken as a regular monthly or quarterly routine it can be spread over a long period.

The best kind of index is a title and subject list with plenty of alternative title entries and with the relevant periodicals listed under the chosen subject headings. Though the work involved in preparing it and keeping it current is considerable, its value in exploiting the resources of a library in which periodical literature plays so important a part is immense.

Periodical files

When released from public service by the substitution of a later issue, a periodical loses none of its importance, for it joins the large numbers on file. All should be kept for at least a year; some will be preserved for varying periods according to need; and many will be bound for permanent file. It is doubtful whether it is worth while to indicate the length of file in the periodical index, which will already be detailed enough. Other records give the information. The permanent runs, which naturally include the most important publications, are catalogued and it is usual, in the larger systems, to compile and keep current an alphabetical union list of periodicals taken in every library, giving

ORGANISATION AND ADMINISTRATION

location and length of file. A copy is held in every department and from it the staff can give accurate information to readers about the system's holdings. It may be thought advisable to compile the additional special list to serve other commercial and technical library purposes recommended later in this chapter. To ensure that numbers released from the public racks are correctly placed, the act of filing should be recorded on a card or slip fixed at the storage point; the slip should also indicate the date when a volume is due for completion so that the binding assistant does not overlook it.

It is sometimes convenient to split the files, keeping certain well-used periodicals near the service point, and placing the remainder in the stack or adjacent store, if there is one. Deep shelving, in tiers 15" wide, prevents copies from becoming mixed, but normal shelving can be used by placing the copies on it longitudinally. There should be a long table near the filing point for sorting each day's returned loose numbers, checking numbers for binding and stripping advertisements from those to be bound skinned. All these daily tasks require a good deal of room and table space; staff time is saved and some errors are avoided if it is provided.

It will only be necessary to bind in full library style periodicals which are to be kept permanently on stock; and even in such cases it may be thought that a cheaper style—possibly in quarter cloth and avoiding the now costly process of lettering in gilt by substituting a typewritten label—will be adequate

COMMERCIAL AND TECHNICAL LIBRARIES

to preserve periodicals which may only be consulted at rare intervals when their contents become outdated. There is no point in incurring the expense of binding those which are to be kept for a few years only. There are several ways of shelving such unbound volumes: they may be kept loose in a box, sewn with string in three or four sections, placed between boards and made into a brown paper parcel, or placed between board covers with a cloth spine and secured with tapes on three sides. Individual ingenuity may suggest other ways.

Directories—arrangement and indexing

Time and labour will be saved if directories and books serving the purpose of directories are arranged and indexed so simply that readers can use them without calling on the services of the staff. In some libraries they are classified by Dewey, but this seems to be an unnecessary and perhaps confusing elaboration. Instead, it may be thought better to arrange them in a number of groups as follows:—British towns (arranged alphabetically); British counties (alphabetically); Commonwealth and foreign (alphabetically by countries); trade directories (in subject groups); telegraphic addresses; and telephone directories. In the case of the trade directories, the order of the subjects, and of individual books in each of them, is not important, The subjects may be placed in alphabetical order, with a general group at the beginning or the end comprising directories

ORGANISATION AND ADMINISTRATION

too wide in scope to come under any one of the subjects chosen. This arrangement enables a reader who finds a trade directory from the index to see others beside it dealing with the same trades. Each directory should carry a large label with its own number clearly marked; numbers should run consecutively throughout the shelves from 1 upwards. Additions can be inserted among those in alphabetical order by adding letters to the preceding numbers; but in the trade directories it may be thought simpler to leave gaps in the number sequences between the subject groupings. This arrangement works well; it avoids the complexities of classification symbols and after reference to the index the reader merely has to identify the only book on the shelves carrying a simple number.

Though directories will be recorded in the catalogue, a handier guide is needed. It is not enough merely to list them by title, or even by the place name, trade or industry appearing in the title, as the information they provide has to be supplemented by year books and other sources the titles of which may not indicate their value or scope as directories. A comprehensive alphabetical index comprising titles, towns, countries, trades, professions, etc., should be compiled from an examination of their contents. Common sense and the types of enquiries received will govern the number and choice of the entries. It is useful to mention specially those giving lists of trade marks, which are often asked for. All such books should be fully recorded under

Commercial Reference Library, Liverpool.

the heading "Trade marks" arranged after the entries of an alphabetised list of the trades and industries covered by them. The fact that a book contains trade marks should also be mentioned in the relevant entries in other parts of the index.

A typewritten loose-leaf index of the kind suggested for periodicals is recommended for this record.

Trade catalogues

In most commercial libraries a collection of trade catalogues has been found useful. All manufacturers are willing to send details of their products to libraries, and circulars sent to firms inviting them to do so will meet with an instant and sometimes overwhelming response.

Trade catalogues are issued in such a variety of sizes and styles that it is not easy to shelve them satisfactorily. Most are small pamphlets, but some are large, heavy handsomely-bound volumes, while a few are little more than leaflets. Perhaps the most practical method is to place them in boxes capable of holding all but the large bound volumes.

Each library must fix the range of its trade catalogues by a system of trial and error, and ruthlessly discard those for which there is no demand. It is doubtful whether the use of an immense collection will ever justify the shelf room it occupies and the time spent on gathering and indexing it.

Most librarians arrange the trade catalogues by subject, with an index of manufacturers' names,

Commercial Library and Information Department, Manchester.

Technical Library, Manchester.

which also contains cross references to articles not adequately indicated under the subject arrangement. Here again, experience is the best guide to the method to be used. One library sorts them alphabetically by names of firms with a full loose-leaf index of subjects. Card indexes are, however, more commonly used. The trade catalogues should be kept current by circularising important firms at regular, but not too frequent, intervals.

Information and other indexes

Special indexes should be compiled to supplement existing sources of information and to provide new ones. Their number and the purposes they are designed to serve will naturally depend on the extent to which the library's stock fails to satisfy enquiries without the creation of such aids. They place on record the results of staff research, and are particularly useful when there are frequent changes of staff. Some of the indexes in use in commercial and technical libraries are mentioned below, but it is not suggested that the librarian should begin to compile similar ones merely because he has not got them; indeed, no special index should be made unless it is known to satisfy a definite want. When it ceases to do so, possibly because the issue of a suitable publication makes it redundant, it should be discarded immediately. As these indexes will not generally be used by the public, the main objection to a card record is removed, and by using $5'' \times 3''$ paper slips, which are cheaper and reduce the number of drawers needed, a substantial saving in cost and space can be made.

The librarian should not hesitate to index freely, but always with practical ends in view. The most important is a general information index; this is essential in every library. Some librarians prefer to make a clippings file instead of a card or slip index; others have both, using the card index for more fugitive items and reserving the clippings file for material relating to more frequent enquiries. An up-to-date clippings file is an effective library show piece; the librarian who can produce for a reader a folder of current information, culled from many sources, experiences a fine sense of achievement, and the reader is (or should be) suitably impressed by the library's efficiency. But the work involved is considerable: files must be weeded as well as built up; and the clippings file, if not sternly controlled, can easily become a monster whose appetite can only be assuaged by the expenditure of an inordinate amount of staff time. It is obviously uneconomic to select, cut out and index material which the librarian thinks *may* be wanted at some time by some reader; a simple card or slip reference does the job more easily and less expensively; but if it is known that constant enquiries are received about certain matters only dealt with in scattered publications there are sound grounds for collecting such items in a clippings file.

The range of the general information index will depend, as always, on readers' needs, but it might well be made really comprehensive. It may comprise (according to the librarian's judgment) items which, in effect, supplement the analyticals in the public catalogue referring to information in new books which is known to interest the library's users; similar entries from periodicals; details of replies to exceptional questions and results of research undertaken; or any other information of this nature. To make weeding simpler, every slip should be dated as it is made. Whether or not certain entries are deemed to be more useful in the public catalogue or the staff index is a matter for decision according to local factors.

Other special indexes should be created when there are sufficient requests for information which cannot be answered from printed sources. For example, one important seaport commercial library has a large index of geographical names, compiled to record variations of, and changes in, the names of foreign places to help exporting firms to find the nearest port to which to direct their wares. It is supplemented by the *Dictionnaire des bureaux de poste*, published by the Union Postale Universelle at Berne (this lists every place in the world with a post office) and the *Official List of Telegraph Offices opened for International Traffic*, issued in Geneva by the General Secretariat of the International Telecommunication Union, both of which are valuable sources for place names. It is also useful to make a special index of publications which regularly print statistics, such as the *Builder*, which provides monthly details of wage rates in the building industry, or *Metal Industry*, in which current prices of non-ferrous metals appear. Some other indexes in use are: world tariffs (some libraries find the *International Customs Journal* and the *Board of Trade Journal* sufficient; others rely on the local chamber of commerce to compile such records); prices and markets reports; commodities (any which enter into world trade, supplementing such works as Brady's *Materials Handbook* and Snell's *Chemicals of Commerce*); commercial cases dealt with in the law reports; commercial associations, federations and unions; cable addresses (supplementing Sell's); local translators; and maps (if all maps are collected from directories and other sources). Not all libraries will want to compile all or perhaps any of these; they are mentioned as examples of special indexes which have been worth while in some library.

In the technical field, it is always useful to index the contents of periodicals for references to or articles on industrial processes on which the literature is scanty, particularly on aspects of research which it is known are being pursued in the works laboratories. The object of such an index is twofold: to supplement the printed cumulated periodical indexes and abstracts by indexing periodicals not included in them, and to bridge the gap between the publication of the article and the issue of the printed index. This is a heavy task which should only be undertaken in rather special circumstances. Constant and careful weeding is obviously required.

ORGANISATION AND ADMINISTRATION

To compile this index, regular and careful checks of the more important periodicals must be made, and the senior assistant who does the work should keep particular watch for announcements and notes about developments which may either affect local industrial processes in being or lead to the introduction of new ones. In connection with this job and many others, it is helpful to make a typewritten alphabetical list of all periodicals taken in the department, ruled to give the normal information previously mentioned (e.g. length of file, period of publication, etc.) and symbols or letters showing in which periodical indexes and abstracts the contents are analysed. It serves several useful purposes. It can be used by new assistants as a simple check list of holdings and their disposition; senior staff dealing with research or special enquiries have in it a ready record of likely sources of information in certain fields; and when index entries of one kind or another are being compiled the list shows how far this is already being done by other agencies. Only those with long experience in the department can remember such details of many hundreds of periodicals, and as in these days there is constant movement among junior assistants, this record, meticulously kept and always current, is an invaluable aid to efficiency.

Enquiries

Answering personal and telephone enquiries is an important part of the service. The majority are simple questions about facts easily collected by comparatively junior staff; the rest vary from those which need for suitable answers a fair knowledge of the book stock allied to experience in enquiry work, to the relatively few which can only be satisfied by a highly-trained librarian with an extensive and detailed knowledge of sources of information in relation to local commerce and industry.

It is useful to keep a record of enquiries, except the simple ones concerned with directory queries or factual information easily culled from well-known quick reference books. The exceptional ones should be recorded on separate forms ruled to give particulars of the enquiry and the source from which the answer was obtained. Those worthy of permanent record should then be carried to the general information index. Questions which cannot be answered satisfactorily should be noted and efforts made to fill the gaps in the library's resources.

Enquirers should not be kept waiting on the telephone when a question cannot be answered quickly. It is more extravagant to do this than to incur the cost of additional outgoing calls, as the instrument is immobilised while the enquirer waits, and in a busy department two or more telephones are in almost constant use. Moreover, business people appreciate efforts to save their time and look upon a return call giving the required information as a compliment to their importance as well as a sign of library efficiency. There should be enough telephone lines to allow quick service.

ORGANISATION AND ADMINISTRATION

As in all reference libraries, the staff will have to search books and other sources to find information for some readers. At what point should the enquirer be asked to make his own search, or even use the library catalogues to find his own material? Of late years this has become a very real problem to librarians. There is a growing tendency on the part of students working on theses to expect the librarian to carry out research for them to a point which clearly goes far beyond what is reasonable. Librarians, with a perhaps mistaken zeal, sometimes go to absurd lengths in providing detailed information for them; by so doing, they are undermining the work of professors and tutors, who often set their students tasks with the express purpose of training them to find and use intelligently the sources of knowledge. For the ordinary reader, unused to books, the librarian might well track down the specific item instead of merely presenting a book to him; but to those whose interests are, or should be, concerned with the gathering of sources, less generous help should be offered. It is enough, in such cases, to indicate and to issue the sources of information; the rest should be done by the reader. Trainee teachers who, when set an essay, calmly write and ask for "information on the trade and industry of ——" should be provided with a list of sources and told to consult them at a library.

It is hard to lay down any rules as so much depends on the nature of the enquiry and the ability and training of the reader. But while the librarian should be a guide to, and an interpreter of, the contents of his library, he should be on his guard against those who take advantage of his professional enthusiasm by trying to use him and his staff as additional clerical assistants.

Many enquiries received at a library which has specialised on the research side will be for articles in periodicals, and in such cases the librarian can legitimately trace them. So many of these requests come in a garbled form, either by errors in the title of the periodical or the date of the article, that his bibliographical skill is needed.

Preparation of bibliographies

If the library grows in public esteem through the range and quality of its work, and becomes known as a source of accurate and current bibliographical and other information in science and technology, it is likely to receive many requests for the preparation of bibliographies and study lists from firms, research workers and individual students. The first two will be dealt with in the next chapter. As regards requests from individual students and readers, the librarian must decide whether they are important enough to justify the amount of work they will cause or whether the particular enquirer is sufficiently knowledgeable to be asked to find his own material. Some such lists are worth doing for their own sake, as once made, they are an addition to the library's resources and their preparation sometimes helps to show deficiencies in the stock. This part of the library's work should be developed as much as possible; it is a splendid form of staff training and education in librarianship. References to important material not on stock should always be included in view of the growing and welcome collaboration between special libraries in the exchange of material for research.

CHAPTER VIII

EXTERNAL ACTIVITIES

THE term "external activities" is used here to cover both the actual services which can be rendered to organisations and groups of library users, and the various forms of direct publicity. It is not easy to dissociate them, for every special service brings the work of the commercial and technical library to the notice of those who will benefit most from using it; for example, a bibliography distributed to members of a technical society or study group is at once a useful way of advertising the library and a valuable and practical aid to the proper use of books.

The truism that good service attracts and retains customers and that bad drives them away applies with equal force to business and libraries. The two have much in common: their problems and the ways of dealing with them are often similar. When the enterprising salesman goes out and secures new clients his firm tries to satisfy them in order to retain their custom; the librarian of the commercial and technical library, too, must take all possible steps to bring the nature of the services he provides before the business and industrial community, and if he arouses their interest, lose no opportunity

EXTERNAL ACTIVITIES

of supplying them with the information and sources they may need.

The extension work of the special department differs from that of a general public library. When a new branch is opened it never lacks readers from among the literate inhabitants of the district it serves; and, as a rule, there is little need for publicity designed to increase the number of its users. A commercial and technical library will also attract students of the subjects covered by its stock, but compared with the immense numbers who use the lending libraries, they are relatively few. Others will come in considerable numbers to consult directories and other quick reference books and to read current periodicals. This "natural" readership is drawn from those who habitually use books, but their number is far below the total of those engaged in business and industry who, if they were fully aware of the value of books as records of experience, could be helped by the library. The general librarian is concerned with readers of all ages and types drawn from the whole population, but the organiser of a special library directs most of his efforts to a limited section, of a generally higher standard of education, whose occupations are more likely to lead to the use of books for practical purposes.

In seeking to bring them to the library, the librarian will face two formidable obstacles. First, those who may already find books essential—as, for example, professional workers—but do not use the public library, are hard to convince that it can help them in their work, for they accept the common fallacy that the public library's concern is the supply of ephemeral books to a large and undiscriminating public. It must be admitted that the poor selection of current scientific and technical books in many public libraries might well lead to such a conclusion. Secondly, other business men, having gained a reasonable competence without using books, see no reason for changing habits which have certainly not retarded their economic development, whatever effect they may have had in other and less obvious ways. So many old established businesses, too, have survived from the spacious days of Victorian industrial supremacy merely by continuing to use well tried methods that their directors do not realise the extent and importance of the remarkable advances in science and technology during recent years. Though industrialists of the more progressive firms have grasped the significance of these changes and have created research and development departments and libraries, many smaller producers still work on lines more suitable to times when the spur of international competition was lacking. It is among these that the librarian will discover his most intractable material.

The commercial and technical librarian should try to reach possible new users of his library by developing a number of projects likely to appeal to them. Normal methods of publicity and advertising are the most obvious ones, but he must be quite certain that the services he offers through them will be able to meet any demands. It is an axiom among publicists that only goods in adequate supply should be advertised. If a new reader is attracted to the department by over-enthusiastic propaganda and finds that it is unable to satisfy his wants, he is unlikely to use it again. In a newly created library, therefore, the librarian should use direct publicity with the utmost caution until he knows that his resources are properly related to the town's needs and that the time is ripe for experiment. It is always useful, and can never be harmful, to provide for the specific wants of individual organisations; but in initial publicity of a more general kind, it is advisable to begin by exploring with care certain sharply defined phases of business and industrial life to which existing library activities may reasonably be directed. On the basis of the experience gained and the new contacts made, stock and services should be built up to allow the department to cater adequately for an ever widening range of satisfied users.

General publicity

A librarian making his first acquaintance with business advertising will be astonished to discover how few commercial publicists have any real regard for the proper use of language or appreciate its importance. The illustrations, expertly done, are usually the core of the work, the letterpress often being added almost as a hurried afterthought. This is probably less a reflection on the standard of literacy of the business man than a recognition of his difficulty in seeing, much less reading, the mass of publicity matter that falls on his desk or, more likely, into the waste paper baskets of his secretarial staff. There can be no doubt that the choice and intelligent use of illustrations and careful balance of colour and of type are the most important adjuncts of any printed publication designed, as it should be, to strike an unexpected or original note in an overcrowded market. If the format has done its job by attracting closer attention, the letterpress then assumes great importance, for it should have been prepared with the object of persuading the reader to try out the service recommended. Apart from all other considerations, no librarian should ever be guilty of publishing anything which is not well written; though the style may perhaps lack grace (for this great and precious gift is vouchsafed to so few!), the English should be grammatically correct.

The invention of new forms of publicity and the exercise of the language of persuasion provide the librarian with an amusing and instructive game outside his normal duties. The principle underlying all such work is first to attract attention, then to convince. It is unwise to write of the library as a "literary" institution in the narrow sense. The failure of public libraries to achieve any place in public esteem may in some measure be due to the tendency of librarians to base what publicity they do on a concept of library values which, even if successfully projected, can only appeal to a small section of the community. In publicising the commercial and technical library the emphasis should be on information rather than books. Books and libraries are associated in most people's minds, and certainly in those of men of commerce and industry, with a world of dreamers and unpractical beings, which is deemed to have no relation to the busy life of hard-headed business men. Publicity for the special library should therefore concentrate on the book as an indispensable tool of commerce and industry, as a record of practical things of value to those engaged in production and distribution. Every opportunity should be taken to call attention to research or information provided by the library which has helped the development of some new process or invention or brought new business to its users.

The first useful step in general publicity may well be to produce a leaflet, carefully phrased, attractively and arrestingly captioned and nicely printed, describing the resources and work of the department. It should be distributed to commercial and industrial establishments—perhaps through the chamber of commerce—and at local conferences and meetings concerned with such matters, and given to all new readers in the library.

It should not be imagined that such a leaflet, however widely it is distributed, will bring an immediate or, indeed, any noticeable response. The

Scientific and Technical Section—Science and Commerce Library, Sheffield.

majority will not be read; some will be read by the wrong people; and the message conveyed by the few which do get into the right hands will probably soon be forgotten. General publicity is a rough and ready method of advertising a highly specialised service and much of it will be wasted; to be effective, its message and presentation must be continually changed and continuously applied. All sorts of attempts to catch the imagination and interest of those whom the commercial and technical library can help should be made at reasonably frequent intervals at a later stage in its development.

Full use should be made of existing publications. The editor of the chamber of commerce journal will doubtless be willing to include a regular monthly note on the library. This could take the form of comments on new activities and special accessions of outstanding importance, or a record of the month's new books. A list of additions, even if annotated with knowledge and imagination, may not arouse excited comment among men of business; the discursive essay form, in which the books are discussed in an interesting way, is perhaps more likely to be read. Records of difficult questions answered provide impressive evidence of the library's range of activities and its staff's competence. Works' magazines are also a fruitful medium for advertising the library. Their editors will usually accept suitable material from a librarian with some gift for writing. All general library publications issued should also include a note on the department. Such references

Science and Commerce Library, Sheffield. Note periodical racks, described in pp. 94–5.

should not be allowed to become routine and be repeated unchanged until their message loses all value; they should be frequently rewritten and their layout recast.

The librarian should not hesitate to follow commercial practice in his efforts to place his goods in the right market; he cannot afford to set himself superior standards and act as if there is something indecent in using the techniques perfected by publicity experts. The most effective form of advertising is the press news item, in which the library's work can be subtly insinuated into a "story" based on an event or a circumstance, perhaps unimportant in itself, but nevertheless possessing the kind of appeal to public interest which the trained journalist at once recognises. For example, the problems the library solves, or the questions the staff answer as a normal routine, always surprise people unfamilar with the work of public libraries. If the press can be persuaded to use some of them, the reporter will almost certainly want to ignore the highly technical queries involving difficult research which give most pride to the librarian, and use some trivial or even silly ones as the main theme of his story. It is wise to allow these to be published if at least one paragraph suggesting a much wider purpose for the library is included. There are immense possibilities of publicity in local newspapers provided that the librarian is prepared to collaborate with them. The really good news story gets the widest publicity of all, and leaves a firm impression on the mind of the reader because, in the hands of a skilled journalist, it arouses interest, the surest spur to action among those whom the general publicity is designed to reach. Should the library be fortunate enough to be in one of the few towns which possess serious newspapers catering for the intelligent few, a different and perhaps more welcome technique can, of course, be adopted.

Useful publicity sometimes comes from the most unexpected quarters. Technical librarians so rarely receive acknowledgments from authors who have been helped by the staff that it is refreshing to find even a mention of what they have done in the preface, and a dedication is an almost miraculous event. Librarians, who have natural human feelings, welcome such acknowledgments because they show that their work is appreciated, and also because they help to extend knowledge of its value among the books' readers. Here are two examples:—

E. Carrington. *Aluminium Alloy Castings*. Griffin, 1946. Preface: ". . . The bibliographies given are largely based upon the excellent Research Bulletin No. 8 Foundry Practice compiled by the City Library of ———."

W. H. Salmon and E. N. Simons. *Foundry Practice*. Pitman, 1951: "Dedicated to the City Librarian and Staff of the Technical Department of the ——— City Library as a slight recognition of the generous and unstinted help given by them to research workers, students, industries and writers."

Recognition of the holdings of certain publications in established libraries is sometimes given by the publishing body; for example, the American Society of Mechanical Engineers records depositories for their *Transactions*.

Newspaper advertisements are costly if they are of sufficient size to be noticed and local authority funds rarely allow much scope for using them. The library should, however, participate in any advertising features in the local press dealing with matters in which it has a legitimate interest, such as technical education or an industrial exhibition. Not less than four or five inches double column should be taken; a lesser size has little value amongst many large ones.

Posters, half-crown or quarter-crown size, drawn by good artists with striking captions, should be distributed to business houses, banks, works, and professional and technical bodies. One produced by the Department of Scientific and Industrial Research sets a useful standard. Other familiar methods of publicity of this kind will suggest themselves to the observant librarian, who must use them according to his knowledge of local conditions.

Book exhibitions and displays

When exhibitions are organised which in any way impinge on the work of the library, it is advisable to try to obtain space for a stand on which a suitable selection of books, periodicals, abstracts, etc., can be displayed, with some pictorial, diagrammatic, or other means of showing how bibliographical services are linked with research and practice. Library material is not in itself very satisfactory for exhibition purposes; to make an outstanding show experts must be called in and considerable sums spent on design, fittings and lighting.

A well-designed exhibit, if it has been planned as a mobile one, can, of course, be used again at little additional cost by merely replacing posters and lettering, which would be necessary in any case to bring the information up to date. If a site for a stand is secured in a large business or industrial exhibition, the librarian should not be disheartened because his own contribution cannot match in cost and magnificence those of exhibitors able to spend large sums on them. No public library can compete at this level, but big exhibitions have such a soporific effect on visitors that a small stand, simply and artistically laid out and carrying a clear and easily understood message, may seem refreshing to the jaded onlooker and be more effective in consequence. The library should be represented as a matter of course at smaller exhibitions organised by local societies and educational bodies concerned with its subjects, and the librarian or one of his staff with a flair for this work might be able to design a useful show piece which could be constructed at little expense. In this case the department's services could be dealt with in more detail because, as the visitors will mainly consist of those already interested in the work of the body concerned and will have less to look at than in large exhibitions, they will probably examine the exhibits more closely.

EXTERNAL ACTIVITIES

As the use of the library grows, it becomes increasingly difficult to release important current material for exhibition purposes, even though arrangements may be made for the immediate return of any item urgently required by a reader, and the librarian may feel that the claims of the service outweigh the publicity value of an exhibition. The use of book jackets and older editions, suitably annotated, may help to overcome this problem.

Displays of books, with attractive posters, designed to draw the attention of the ordinary "single track" borrower to subjects and departments he does not normally think of using, are now recognised elements in library method, and whatever use can be made of them by the commercial and technical library should be carefully considered. The librarian should be on the lookout for new accessions likely to be overlooked by the ordinary commercial reader: the *Hints to Business Men* series, the International Bank reports, the Colonial Office reports, are cases in point. More fruitful ventures in display work, however, are those arranged in the entrance hall of the central library, or perhaps, in suitable fittings, in the lending library. Readers of scientific and technical literature in the lending library should be told, by small notices suitably sited on the shelves, that if the book they want is "out", a copy may be available for immediate study in the commercial and technical department. In some towns the owners of an adjoining building heavily used, such as a taxation office, an employment exchange, or a museum, might allow small case displays of books, which could be easily fetched when required by readers. Considerable ingenuity and a quick appreciation of possibilities are required by the librarian of such a department who thinks of making much use of display work.

Extension work of the kinds mentioned opens up new spheres of interest and activity to the enterprising librarian, and also gives him opportunities of making new contacts and improving old ones. The immediate results of these efforts, which absorb a great deal of time and energy, and sometimes unduly excite the imagination, will probably seem disappointing to the enthusiast. The effect of publicity of all kinds can never be judged by specific responses, which are understandably few; if intelligently done, however—and whatever methods he adopts to attract attention, the librarian should always be careful not to claim for his library virtues and powers it does not possess—the cumulative effect is considerable. Continuous propaganda, backed by good service, gradually builds up the acceptance of an idea, though its extent can rarely be measured.

Special contacts

One obvious form of specially directed publicity can be safely undertaken immediately the library is created. A list of directories and codes, either printed or stencilled, should be circulated to all commercial houses. It is not necessary to spend time,

EXTERNAL ACTIVITIES

labour and money in producing an elaborate printed subject list; a simpler, briefer record is more likely to invite attention. It is presumed, of course, that a commercial and technical library would not be opened unless it possessed a reasonable range of such books.

Similar approaches can be made, as opportunity offers, to other sections of library users. The fact that there are holdings of British (in deposit libraries) and foreign patent publications and specifications of standards should be widely circulated, and the accession of special collections, such as the deposit of a set of the reports of the United States Atomic Energy Commission in one commercial and technical library, should be notified to suitable libraries and to works research and development departments in the area. The issue of brief notes on important additions, directed to those likely to be interested, can be carried out in a wide variety of ways at little expense.

The librarian should give personal contacts a high place in his public relations service. He should keep in close touch with foreign consular officials, by whom he will be kept informed of their countries' publications and probably be given free copies of the more important of them. It is sometimes possible to obtain supplementary sources of directory information by this means, even if only in the form of telephone directories. In any case, every effort should be made to see foreign governments' official publications concerned with trade, with which

COMMERCIAL AND TECHNICAL LIBRARIES

the consul will naturally be familiar. A consul is merely doing his job by keeping the library informed of his country's activities, but he must be convinced that it is worth while to do so; if he becomes interested in the library he can be useful in a number of ways, notably in making translations of matter in little known languages.

Enquiries are often received, particularly in connection with marketing research, which involve knowledge of current local employment statistics not available in print. A helpful manager of the Ministry of Labour Employment Exchange may provide them if the right approach has been made to him.

The director or secretary of the chamber of commerce is another vital link in the library's chain of external services. The more efficient chambers sometimes maintain important records, such as a card index of customs and tariffs of all countries; and if the librarian can have access to them there is obviously no point in duplication. They also provide information services to members. Some are content to rely on the library for much of the information they give, and acquire merit by proxy, as it were; with others an effective liaison can be established by which the chamber and the library supplement each other's sources of information to their mutual satisfaction. Whatever the standard of its activities, the chamber is a valuable point of contact with the local business world. Another new and important organisation is the local Productivity Committee.

EXTERNAL ACTIVITIES

Apart from the general co-ordination of book and periodical holdings in the area, which will be dealt with later, the librarian should be at pains to establish good relations with his colleagues at the university library. There is no point in both libraries buying expensive sets of publications for which requests may be few such as, for example, the *Transactions of the Newcomen Society*. Provided that the university librarian will allow readers recommended by the commercial and technical librarian access to them, the money saved can be spent to better advantage on other books of importance to the area as a whole. This applies also to other near-by libraries. There are, of course, many other useful forms of collaboration between the two institutions.

When the library has built up its stock and acquired some local prestige, it will be found that the scientific and technical staffs of the university and the colleges of commerce and technology become regular users of it. As their help in book selection is often invaluable, their interest in the library should be encouraged. For example, it is most useful to have at hand a trusted and disinterested specialist to advise on such difficult matters as the extent to which the library should stock books dealing with specialised functions in higher mathematics. Apart from this, as they are engaged in training young scientists and technicians, their interest helps to develop one of the most fruitful activities of the library.

COMMERCIAL AND TECHNICAL LIBRARIES

Education in library use

The value of talks to societies and groups about the library service has always been realised by librarians, who give many hours of precious private time to this kind of elementary missionary work. Speakers dealing with the general library service often find that most of their hearers are already borrowers, for people keen enough on things of the mind to attend talks on libraries are usually good readers. Even among such audiences, however, comparatively few know the full value of the service given by a commercial and technical library. It is therefore always worth while both for the librarian to give talks on his own work, and for other library speakers on the service in general to devote some of their time to the department.

Library visits of societies, particularly those concerned with professional and technical education, and other groups and classes, are even more valuable; and their secretaries should be freely invited to organise them. The librarian should not hesitate to provide time to arrange visits from pupils of the secondary modern schools, for though the limits of a cursory talk about the library are obvious, in such cases the young people leave with at least some understanding of the fact that a public library is concerned with practical ends as well as with what is loosely called "culture". If there is a system of training school leavers in the use of books and libraries in collaboration with the education authority (as there should be in every town), part

EXTERNAL ACTIVITIES

of the syllabus of instruction and practice should deal with some elementary books in the commercial and technical library. The justification for this activity, which to the busy librarian may seem to be an unwelcome addition to his other duties, is to be found in the trite phrase, so popular with public representatives on educational platforms, "The childdren of today are the citizens of tomorrow". The profundity of the thought may not move us, but its practical implications have value.

A start with a more rewarding method might well be made by applying a carefully prepared system of training in the use of books to the pupils of the college of commerce, who, being older and under training in a specific course, are likely to be much more receptive than secondary modern school pupils. Those with long experience of class visits realise that a talk about the library and its organisation, usually confined to a description of the classification and the catalogue, followed by an inspection, is not really adequate. The best way to instruct pupils in the use of books is to get them to use books. If a series of questions, each carefully chosen to excite curiosity and each capable of being answered from books, is prepared, the young people who use them to provide the answers are likely to retain a vivid memory of what certain books can do. The classes should be spread over a period, so that the pupils will have time to work through representative types of books. The introductory talk before the actual practice should be limited to a brief description of the books chosen for the lesson and the purposes each of them serves. For a commercial course of this nature, as carried out each year in one commercial and technical library, the practice books comprise each type of directory, codes, and certain well-known annuals and year books; some books must, of course, be "planted" so as to provide coverage to the questions set.

Ideally, of course, such lessons should be a regular part of the normal educational courses. It is unfortunate that young people leave colleges of commerce knowing little of the importance of the book as a tool of business; but it is impossible for the normal staff and finances of a public library to cope with a really full scheme for such training, if it is applied, as it should be, to all senior pupils in commerce, science and technology. It would need, for its successful operation, one or more tutors with experience in both teaching and librarianship. The work of preparing the hundreds of questions set—for each paper must be different—and the subsequent checking of them, is enormous. In a limited scheme, such as the one briefly described, the staff of the commercial and technical library may be able to squeeze it in with their normal work; but if the classes were to be extended as suggested in the next chapter, the additional cost would have to be a charge on education. The collaboration of the library staff, who are familiar with sources and commercial and industrial trends, would be needed, but whatever scheme is devised should not be allowed to interfere with their primary duty of maintaining the quality of the library service.

Even if carried out on a limited scale, such training helps the librarian to build up a new and valuable readership. It has been in operation in one commercial and technical library for twenty years, and the heavy use of the quick reference commercial section of that library is probably largely a result of the systematic practice young people obtain in the use of business books.

Bibliographies and study lists

A close link can be forged with institutions concerned with formal education by supplying bibliographies for their classes, and the limit to this kind of collaboration need only be set by the requirements of the tutors and lecturers and the time the librarian is able to give to the work. The issue of bibliographies can be extended to other classes arranged by research and trade associations, professional bodies, the National Trades Technical Societies, the University Extra-Mural Department, and to special courses dealing with relevant subjects such as some of those organised by the Ministry of Education.

In selecting books for class lists, the librarian should recognise his limitations by inviting the specialists who ask for them to assist in their preparation. If it is to serve its purpose, a study list for a course of lectures should consist of books chosen from the library stock by the lecturer himself, for he alone knows how he intends to deal with his subject. It is best first to discuss the syllabus with the lecturer in order to gain a general idea of the scope; the librarian should then collect the material available in the library and invite the lecturer to make his choice from it. By this means a really useful bibliography can be made, for it will include only books actually related to the course of study, whereas, if the librarian makes the selection himself, he may often refer students to books later found to be unsuitable. Moreover, the librarian's book knowledge is broadened by discussing the literature of a subject with a knowledgeable person, and in the course of this close association the lecturer may be able to point out deficiencies in the library's stock without feeling that he may give offence by doing so. This is one of the most effective ways of building up a library to serve the known needs of the community. Few helpful contacts of this kind can be made with individual readers, because the librarian will probably find that many book recommendations received from such a source reflect too personal a point of view.

The main library will probably possess either an electric rotary duplicator or some other machine by which enough copies of a bibliography can easily be made to supply each student with one. Lecturers rarely have access to copying facilities and warmly welcome a service which costs little and puts into the hands of hundreds of keen students a splendid testimony to the library's efficiency. The extent to which work of this kind can be carried out is shown by the issue by one commercial and technical library of nearly 10,000 foolscap sheets of study lists for a winter's lecture courses of a large trades technical organisation. When the knowledge spreads that the library is willing to provide bibliographies on this scale, interest in its work is widened and its prestige as an active and competent adjunct of technical education is greatly enhanced.

Similar lists should be prepared, when required, for professional societies, which often have student bodies and arrange courses of lectures for them. Those concerned with accountancy, engineering, mining and the new and popular study of management, for example, are active in promoting technical study, and even municipal officers have been known to take some sporadic interest in the advancement of knowledge of local government. Should it happen that a large professional society has a secretary who, by personality and enthusiasm, has aroused a rare educational fervour among the membership, it may be an economic proposition to print a general reading list for the profession. The numbers justify the extra cost and it always looks nicer.

A library which gives this service will receive requests for bibliographies from the research departments of local firms and from interested persons in firms too small to undertake the costly process of organised research. These latter are mainly concerned with practice and production, but their purpose is no less vital to the country's productivity. All reasonable needs of industrial organisations should be met. When preparing bibliographies for them there is even more reason to work in close collaboration with the experts concerned, whether they be research scientists or departmental managers, for no librarian, whatever his scientific training, can possibly be fully conversant with the shifting trends of industrial production. A bibliography prepared on these lines will be authoritative, and might well be issued to a wider public, both through British and foreign research organisations and to individuals. Work of this kind can only be undertaken in a commercial and technical library in close touch with industry, possibly through the kind of interchange organisation briefly described later in this chapter. A good deal of work is involved, but there are compensations in that institutions which receive the bibliographies reciprocate by sending their own publications. For example, in a commercial and technical library where this form of specialisation has reached an advanced stage, valuable bibliographies have been received in exchange from the Special Libraries Association of America and from the Verein Deutscher Eisenhüttenleute. No better way of removing the misunderstanding about the scope and purpose of public libraries can be devised than these widely distributed records of their ability to play an important part in the national campaign for technical efficiency. If the lists are competently done they are eagerly sought after. One recently issued on a new and

EXTERNAL ACTIVITIES

important casting process was asked for by over 300 organisations and firms from all over the world.

There may be occasions when the production of a larger printed bibliography, dealing with a range of subjects in connection with a national event concerned with trade or industry, is worth while. Such opportunities are rare; the work involved in the preparation of elaborate lists and the cost of printing them are heavy; and it is not easy to find suitable methods of distribution. In the commercial and technical library larger printed bibliographies are of doubtful value, except to other librarians and bibliographers. The same amount of effort devoted to smaller lists prepared for specific groups of readers who ask for them is much more rewarding.

Opinions differ about the value of a regular bulletin issued to firms and library users. If printed, they are costly to produce, and some librarians question whether the time spent on them is justified in towns where the information officers of the main industrial establishments already circulate among their many departments skilfully prepared bulletins of references to and abstracts of material dealing with their research and production activities. A library publication of this kind can only be general in scope because it caters for many firms making a variety of products; it is difficult for a public librarian to produce useful references covering so wide a range of interests. If distributed free, they are likely to share the common fate of all general publications.

COMMERCIAL AND TECHNICAL LIBRARIES

A recently created technical library has approached the distribution problem in a novel way. Its monthly *Documents Bulletin*, which lists the preceding month's accessions, and provides relevant annotations of the books, titles of the more important articles in the periodicals, and patents information, is produced by a cheaper photographic process and is issued on a small subscription basis. This reduces the cost of publication and limits the distribution to firms and libraries whose appreciation of its value is shown by the continuance of their subscriptions.

Research establishments and their workers—an interchange scheme

The stock of the technical sections of most joint libraries will probably consist mainly of standard books and periodicals, but certain industries may be of such prime importance in the town that a high degree of specialisation can be reached in the literature about them. In such a case it is possible to treat on equal terms with the industrial research and development departments and their librarians or information officers, and to work out methods of collaboration which may ultimately result in the commercial and technical library becoming the recognised information centre for the industries.

If well stocked and administered, it is peculiarly fitted for this role, but it cannot perform it unless the confidence of industrialists has been obtained. Much will depend, too, on the number and quality of research libraries in the area. If there are some

EXTERNAL ACTIVITIES

good libraries of institutions and large firms with efficient research and development departments, the basic conditions for close co-ordination of certain activities are present; smaller organisations can be brought in later. The librarian of an active commercial and technical library will already have gained the goodwill of his colleagues in research and industrial libraries by identifying and obtaining material which they have not been able to get from the sources open to them. It takes at least three days and often much longer for loans from distant centres to reach the applicant. As the material may be wanted quickly in connection with a problem that has arisen in a production process, it would obviously be helpful if the publication could be obtained locally. It may already be stocked at another library in the area; and it is a short step to realise that if all this material were pooled and made available through a well-planned system of interchange, it could be used with a minimum of delay.

The initial move in the creation of an organisation to do this work will fall on the public library, which is not without some responsibility in the matter, since the welfare of the local authority depends on the success of the town's industries. The librarian should convene a conference of directors of research, librarians, technical information officers and others likely to be interested. To give suitable standing to the meeting and to offset any misunderstandings about the public library's place in such a scheme, a chairman whose importance in industrial circles will guarantee a representative attendance should be obtained.

The convener of the conference would be well advised to prepare a memorandum outlining a scheme for consideration at this meeting, for there is probably no more futile instrument than a committee without a guiding mind. The submission should deal with general principles only; what is needed at this stage is a resolution in the form of a kind of general blessing which will commit those in a position to do so to give authority to their firms' representatives to take part in the organisation. The main function of the conference is to launch the scheme and appoint a small committee to work out the details.

The librarian of the commercial and technical library should not be surprised to find that he will be expected to be its administrator; as his organisation will probably be the largest in it and must make the greatest contribution, it is desirable that direction and control, subject to the general views of other members, should be in his hands. In any case, the librarian's experience in working with voluntary organisations will have taught him that everything depends on the enthusiasm and application of a few people, for talkers are many, but willing, competent workers are hard to find.

It is well to begin by planning a workable method for the interchange of books and periodicals in the libraries of members. The organisation should be simple, and the rules should be the minimum

EXTERNAL ACTIVITIES

required to work the scheme. Ambitious plans for complete union catalogues which figure so much in librarians' dreams should find no place in it. If they achieve the rare distinction of being accurate and current, they record, at great expense of time, money and energy, the existence of masses of little used books and the fact that the stocks of many libraries are very similar. The larger member libraries will not have the staff, and certainly not the inclination, to copy all their records. Centralised records of some kind must, of course, be made. Holdings of periodicals are so important that a complete union list of them should be compiled by distributing 5" × 3" printed slips to members on which they can record their periodicals and the extent of the files. These should be checked and amended where necessary (many who submit them will have had little or no library experience and inaccuracies and inconsistencies will be numerous) and then alphabetised. It may be thought desirable to prepare and issue to members copies of the union list, with adequate space for additions and amendments, but so many changes have to be made under present conditions of periodical publishing that its value in relation to the time spent by all concerned in keeping it current is debatable. The rules should provide for the regular notification to headquarters of alterations in members' holdings. A telephone request for an item can then be checked by the union list. If the periodical is available through the interchange, the enquirer is notified of its location, and the actual exchange carried out direct between the members concerned.

For books, all that is needed is to record those in the small collections, which are often of a specialised kind. The nature of the book stocks of research association, institution and other special libraries will generally be obvious from the scope of their work; those of the larger works libraries will mainly duplicate that of the commercial and technical department. Its catalogue will thus be a reasonable guide to the general scientific and technical literature in the area. It is easy to check with member libraries over the telephone when requests for books not stocked at headquarters are received, and if all enquiries satisfied in this way are recorded, a small union catalogue of books outside the normal range of stock can be created with little trouble.

It should be a basic condition of membership that a suitable contribution is made to the common pool. Firms, like individuals, vary in outlook; while some are willing and helpful, others may try to take out more than they are prepared to put in. Though contributions and use can never be equated, nor is it desirable to attempt to do so, some minimum standard of holdings of books and periodicals should be laid down. It should be comparatively low, for a small but highly specialised research organisation or a minor firm making a rare product may be able to provide material which, though small in bulk, has great value. For example, in one such interchange organisation, a radio-therapy research

EXTERNAL ACTIVITIES

centre with a tiny library provides some files of periodicals and research publications sometimes wanted by physicists engaged in metallurgical research involving the use of X-rays and radioactive isotopes. On the other hand, a large works library may have several thousand books and hundreds of periodicals, most of which are already in stock in the commercial and technical library and are useful only as duplicates. On balance, it would seem that the smaller collection is the more useful of the two. It is essential to fix a standard to avoid embarrassment, but the criterion for admission to membership should rest mainly on the quality rather than the quantity of the material the new member is able to offer.

The other conditions under which such an organisation is run must be framed in accordance with local circumstances and need not be detailed here. Some general observations may, however, be helpful to those contemplating the creation of one.

It is almost inevitable that the bulk of the borrowings will be from the commercial and technical library, which must be prepared to lend to members. It is important to lay down conditions that make it possible for any material so lent to be returned within a short time. Lending should be to firms for research and practice in the works, and not to individuals, who can use the library for private study on precisely the same terms as other readers. There is no reason why they should be put in a privileged position. Every loan should remain on the firm's premises

COMMERCIAL AND TECHNICAL LIBRARIES

during normal opening hours so that it can be returned by car on request. This, in turn, sets a limit to the area in which the organisation can operate, apart from the fact that as speed is its keynote, the great majority of borrowings will be made by messenger.

Under such a scheme, the local authority will bear the cost of administration, which is considerable, though there are compensations in that the public library is allowed to borrow from members material wanted by its own readers. The local authority can reasonably be expected to make its special services to commerce and industry as productive as possible in this way, but when applications for membership are received from places some fifteen to twenty miles away—which is probably the practical distance limit for an interchange run on these lines—the libraries committee must decide as a matter of principle whether it is prepared to accept them. Public libraries are provided wholly out of local rates for the education and entertainment of the people of the area governed by the local authority. Certain services, such as the reference libraries and archive collections, are open to all scholars and students. The reasons for this are partly administrative, because of the difficulty of trying to distinguish between residents and non-residents, and partly because the larger towns accept some responsibility for the welfare of the areas of which they are the centres and from which they draw some of their wealth. These arguments can legitimately be used

EXTERNAL ACTIVITIES

for extending the privileges of the interchange scheme to firms outside the town.

Once the organisation is in being, the exchange of pooled material will become a simple, easily administered routine for the bulk of the material lent, but some enquiries will tax the resources of the library and the abilities of the librarian and his senior staff. If, as will probably be the case, some research libraries are members of it, their librarians will be familiar with the normal bibliographical tools and may only use the public library when their own records fail or when the enquiry is outside the normal range of their interests. Other special requests for information will be received from firms which have little knowledge of library practice and rely on the commercial and technical library to find sources of information for them and help in their use. It will therefore be clear that when a library undertakes the administration of an interchange organisation, it naturally becomes a scientific and technical information centre for the district. It should, of course, try to fulfil this function in any case, but it will be helped to do so more effectively under these conditions.

The commercial and technical library should have at its command every possible bibliographical aid likely to be of service to the industries of the area. It should be a member of all associations and institutions concerned with them, including foreign (particularly American) ones. It must also build up friendly reciprocal relations with other specialised libraries so that exchanges of material can be made quickly. As the interchange develops, the members themselves will be able to add to the resources of the headquarters library. Many works information officers provide stencilled abstracts of periodicals and research publications for their departments, and are usually willing to send copies for cutting and mounting on cards at headquarters; translations, including the invaluable Brutcher publications, are also generally made available; some, lacking room, are glad to present files of important periodicals for permanent preservation; and works' librarians often call attention to important publications or to forthcoming technical developments which the commercial and technical librarian might otherwise have missed.

The benefits the commercial and technical library receives in exchange for the responsibility of administering an efficient system of interchange are considerable. Constant contact with colleagues working in close touch with production helps the librarian to obtain a more informed knowledge of the literature of local industries. He is able to note the trends of production, and stock his library accordingly. If he has doubts about the authority of any publication or its usefulness, or if he has a particularly tough query to deal with involving specialised scientific or technical experience which no librarian can possess, he has at his service a helpful panel of experts, one of whom is usually able to resolve his difficulty either by himself or in consultation with a colleague. This highly competent assistance is also at the librarian's disposal when he is preparing bibliographies on some aspects of research or production.

It will be seen that the simple act of interchanging published material may well develop into an organised system in which all the scientific and technical information resources of an area are available through the commercial and technical library. As the quality of its service grows, it becomes more than a local centre; it gradually acquires national recognition as a place where accurate information on those industries can be obtained, and libraries and firms throughout the country and abroad use it for this purpose. Its strength as a reliable source lies in the fact that under these conditions it is not a mere paper organisation; it is backed by the applied skill and knowledge of able men and women actually working in the industries, who are able to bring to the solution of any problem a judgment tempered by experience of the application of practice to theory.[1]

A co-operative plan for London

The division of the London area into a number of comparatively small local authorities makes it difficult for any one public library to create a commercial and technical library on the lines of those

[1] For details of the organisation and administration of an interchange system such as the one briefly described, the reader is referred to Lamb, J. P. "The interchange of technical publications in Sheffield", *ASLIB Proceedings*, Vol. 2, 1950, pp. 41–48.

provided by the large provincial cities; and the variety of the lighter industries and their widespread location are an additional handicap. In these circumstances, such work can probably best be done through the co-operation of a number of libraries. An organisation on these lines was first suggested in 1950, and ten public libraries in West London evolved a scheme known as the Co-operative Industrial and Commercial Reference and Information Service (CICRIS).

Each library undertakes to specialise in an agreed technical field for books, periodicals and other printed material, and to make contact with other sources of information in its selected subjects. Industrial firms, technical college libraries and research organisations have agreed to lend material within the area covered.

In general, the organisation operates on much the same principles as the one previously mentioned. It already has considerable achievements to its credit and is still growing. The normal difficulties to be found in any voluntary co-operative system—the uneven nature of individual effort and enthusiasm and the tendency for the heavy work involved to be laid on the shoulders of the willing few—are perhaps increased in this case by the fact that more "supplying" libraries take part in it.

The success of this project, which is admirably designed to overcome the problems peculiar to the London area, is already stimulating other parts of the metropolis to organise similar ones.

CHAPTER IX

THE FUTURE

THE future of commercial and technical libraries will be profoundly affected by the emphasis now being placed on scientific and technical education and practice. It is taking several forms: the erection and enlargement of colleges of commerce, science and technology; the expansion of the university science and technical departments; government projects for establishing a science centre to act as a national reference library of scientific and technical literature and for creating or developing agencies for the dissemination of technical information; and the encouragement being given to industry to establish libraries and research departments closely integrated with the work of the research associations.

All are likely to add to the number of readers of scientific and technical literature, and all will have some influence on the work of the commercial and technical library. Though so far its place in the national plan is as insignificant as public librarians have learned from experience to expect, the developments now taking place and the proposals still under discussion should be examined in relation to the problems the commercial and technical library has to face. An attempt will be made to do so in this chapter.

The public library suffers from certain disabilities some of which are inherent in its history. Though it has pioneered many schemes which show how readily an institution so closely in touch with the lives and interests of the people can interpret the significance of social, economic and educational trends at an early stage, it has never received national recognition. The ideas conceived and nurtured in public libraries have later been adopted and developed by other agencies which, though they may not have been as effective instruments for applying them, had the advantage of support from national funds and had acquired a greater share of public esteem. There seems little reason to doubt that the work of commercial and technical libraries will share the same fate. Their librarians may well ask: why has this department, which in some towns has been of outstanding value to industrial research and production, made so little impression on those charged with the duty of making recommendations for a national plan?

One reason undoubtedly is the predominantly local character of the public library. One of the oldest of the municipal services, its powers have scarcely changed since it first began to provide books for instruction and entertainment a century ago, and as it is wholly dependent on municipal finance, most of its activities are naturally confined to its own community. While certain other muni-

THE FUTURE

cipal departments are thought to be of such national importance that some form of central control or direction is deemed desirable—which in turn means grants from national funds—the public library has been left to develop according to the economic status of the local authority, the value it places on the importance of books, and the energy or laxity, competence or ineptitude, of the responsible officer. As a result, the services of different authorities are of a very uneven standard, and claims which may justly be made for one efficient organisation are found to be inapplicable to others. An examination of a particular aspect of the service throughout the country gives such unbalanced results that those who make it are perhaps not unreasonable in doubting the effectiveness of special departments or, indeed, of public libraries as a whole. Another reason for their neglect at national level probably lies in the fact that the metropolitan libraries are regarded as representative by those who have no experience of the composite and highly developed activities with which the large city systems serve the bibliographical needs of the community. Research workers in the metropolis have access to so many reference and special libraries that there is not the same pressure on the borough libraries to create commercial and technical libraries or other specialised services like those of the cities in that remote and largely undiscovered part of Britain situate to the north of Waltham Abbey Cross.

Local control exercised without the stimulus of

national grants and the influence of a policy-making central authority has resulted in library finances being quite insufficient for their potentialities and rarely adequate for the more urgent needs. The demands made on the public library are so many and varied that, in seeking to meet all of them—for it is very vulnerable to local criticism—it has been compelled to spread its slender resources so widely that it has succeeded in really satisfying none. For example, the weight of popular reading is so heavy, and the cost of the books, staff and buildings needed to cope with it absorbs so large a part of the income, that none but the largest and most prosperous systems are able to provide adequate stocks of books on advanced aspects of science and technology as well. In places where the reference departments are well stocked and the very costly process of keeping up to date a large collection of scientific and technical literature is attempted, it may have to be done at the expense of other branches of the service, as is shown by the expenditure on books in certain of the large city systems in relation to the number of libraries they maintain.

It is against this background that the future of commercial and technical libraries must be considered. If some of them have failed to reach a high standard of service, the fault lies not so much in their organisation or the ideas and hopes of those who administer them, as in factors over which neither the committee nor the librarian has any control. Yet, despite the difficulties, most of them have succeeded in establishing valuable and productive contacts with industry. They override local criticism and finance by serving a much wider area than the boundaries of their authority; indeed, at least one such library has gone further and has become recognised as a national centre for sources and for information on certain aspects of industrial research and practice. There are obvious limits to the use of local funds for such activities, which should attract government support. It can be argued that if some libraries can do work of national importance, there is no reason why others, if adequately financed, should not do so well. The fact that the technical departments of public libraries are likely to find only a very minor place in the proposed national plan for the provision of scientific and technical information is further evidence that their long history as a purely local service has made it difficult for those unaware of recent developments to see them in any other role.

It is probable that the creation of secondary modern and secondary technical schools and the erection of colleges of commerce, science and technology will result in a large increase in the numbers of pupils wanting elementary, intermediate and sometimes advanced scientific and technical books. The expansion of the university departments of science and technology will also produce more students of degree and research standard. Though the libraries of all these institutions will naturally be expanded accordingly, many students will also use the public library, and it will be almost the only source of books available to them when their training ends. It is therefore important to consider, in the first place, how to meet this new challenge in the commercial and technical library, for it will certainly place new burdens on its book stock and accommodation. It is, in fact, already a pressing problem in some of them.

THE COMMERCIAL LIBRARY

An efficiently administered commercial library will have attracted most firms and persons likely to make regular use of it, and while every opportunity should be taken to make it even more widely known, there is unlikely to be any considerable expansion of its work among those engaged in commerce. It seems equally unlikely that developments in commercial education will place an unbearable burden upon it. Though many users live outside the boundaries of the authority it still remains, in essence, a local service. The large municipalities, in which alone an advanced library of this type is able to justify its existence, have little difficulty in maintaining the stock and service at a high pitch of excellence; and such a library can work effectively with little help in book loans from other libraries. All such libraries are successfully performing a most valuable function for an important, though numerically small part of the community, without undue strain on municipal finances, and there seems no reason why they should not continue to do so.

THE FUTURE

THE TECHNICAL LIBRARY

The case of the technical or scientific and technical library is different. It is much more heavily used for study than the commercial library, and experience proves that there seem to be few limits to the demands which a really active department of this kind can stimulate. The accession of large numbers of new students will tax its resources to the utmost for, proportionately to other classes of books, scientific and technical literature is costly, particularly as many important works are American. Moreover, as the technical library has previously catered mainly for advanced students and those few technical workers sufficiently interested in their job and their own future to undertake intensive study, its seating accommodation is usually not large. Unless much larger premises for a greatly expanded service can be envisaged, including a students' room for those engaged in advanced study and research, it may become necessary to review the principles on which its organisation is based.

Younger students, except the most ambitious and gifted among them, will normally not be attracted to the technical library, but since some text-books on local trades and on workshop practice are usually stocked, a number of them may use it in preference to the lending departments if the libraries of the educational institutions do not wholly satisfy them. The librarian may therefore have to discourage them by raising the minimum standard of books provided and by suspending some of the activities described in the previous chapter, such as the form of training in book use designed to stimulate the interest of the brighter pupils of the secondary modern schools. Those whose education has not advanced beyond the stage when their studies are largely confined to set text-books could be catered for by enlarging the stocks of elementary and intermediate books in the home reading libraries and by heavy duplication of those in common use. The purpose of these suggestions is to ease any possible pressure on the technical department and not to evade the public library's clear duty of providing suitable books for all classes of readers. Separating readers and books into types which will have a mutual attraction is the only practical way of dealing with diverse reading needs. There are obvious difficulties in carrying out such a plan, as the technical library cannot exclude books needed by adult technicians who wish to study their trades or to find ways of removing snags encountered in the workshop. Nevertheless, if the problem is tackled with imagination and skill, it should be possible to divert many readers from the technical library to other branches of the service. Its use by advanced students could also be partially reduced in the same way, though many of them will want a true reference library. If books are needed in the quantities anticipated, there is every reason for heavily duplicating in home reading libraries all books except those of a purely reference character and those which the technical librarian readily recognises as "specialised".

THE FUTURE

The only reader left to be considered is the younger student who, for domestic or other reasons, wishes to study in a library. His case could be met by increasing the proportion of books on practical subjects in the reference sections of branches where there is a reference library or a study room. This has already been done in a new branch library of a city with a highly developed central technical department.

Relations with technical education

As the libraries of the technical education institutions grow, the technical librarian should keep in close touch with the work of his professional colleagues who administer them. It is to be hoped that at an early stage in their development they will be staffed by trained and adequately paid librarians, for they should be linked up in every possible way with the class teaching and workshop practice carried out in the institutions.

The need to avoid unnecessary and costly overlapping in the provision of expensive and little used books will not be lessened when several technical libraries serve the same area for different purposes. The full requirements of readers can rarely be satisfied by any library, and money saved by co-ordinated book selection can be put to better use. How far collaboration in book purchase and exchange can be carried out must be decided in the light of events. There are many other ways in which frank exchanges of views about common problems could be mutually advantageous. If one of the major educational libraries creates an index of special material or a general index of periodical contents, the commercial and technical librarian would find it helpful to have access to it, and vice versa. Joint book exhibitions could be arranged; loans of books could be made from one to the other for special purposes, as, for example, when the college library is supporting a study course by books as well as by book lists. Alternatively, the public library holdings might be included in the lists to show students where they can have access to additional sources, though these would mainly consist of books in the home reading libraries. All the educational libraries should be members of the district interchange scheme.

It has been suggested that the more elementary system of training in book use applied to younger students should be suspended in the technical library; but if the library is extensively used by others progressing to research standard there are sound reasons for providing courses of training for them in the use of the bibliographical tools of research. Knowledge of sources will be essential to them during their studies under instruction and when they become practising research workers. There is an important difference between the education of students of humane subjects and of science and technology. The training of the former encourages them to read widely outside their set books, and this usually involves some understanding of library practice. The scientific and technical student, on the other hand, largely confines himself to mastering the standard text-books set for him and rarely needs to look beyond them until he has passed on to higher levels of study.

It is therefore desirable that the more advanced students should receive special training in the recognition and use of sources. This is primarily a matter for the educational authorities, for at the student stage it can only be properly carried out by lecturers and tutors working on special study courses; in any case, the technical librarian could not possibly find the time to undertake regular extraneous duties of this kind. Some part of the advanced training should take place in the technical library, where it is to be expected that the widest range of sources will be found, except perhaps in the university library.

Librarians are fully aware of the importance of such training. The number of students of near degree standard who do not know how to use libraries and bibliographies is astonishing; and it is to be hoped that educationalists will one day realise that it is an essential part of their job to train them to do so. If more users of the technical library could find their own sources, the staff time saved could be put to better use.

Many of those who accept posts in industry will continue their studies in the technical library; they must keep abreast of developments through books, periodicals and specialist publications; and every opportunity should therefore be taken, preferably in their later student years, to make them fully aware of its scope and activities. This can best be done by applying to older students a carefully planned and co-ordinated system of training in the use of books and libraries, and by linking up as far as possible the services of the technical library and its educational counterparts.

Relations with research establishments

It is presumed that the technical librarian will already have built up a co-operative system of exchange of material and information with those engaged in industrial research and practice like the one described in the last chapter. His library will have become an administrative centre for tracing sources and supplying specialised publications; and though this will be a many sided arrangement—for the exceptional knowledge and experience of his colleagues in different industries and research establishments are equally a part of the district organisation—he will be expected, as a public servant, to carry the main burden. The phenomenal growth in the number of highly complex enquiries received in technical libraries during recent years may have reached a point almost of embarrassment in view of financial limitations. If the library, by outstanding work in this field, achieves national or international recognition as a reliable source of information on certain subjects, the number of enquiries may become so great that some

THE FUTURE

limit must be set to them. The main pressure will be on staff, which is costly in relation to observable results, for some enquiries entail many hours of search. In such circumstances local interests must have priority; but even if all requests from outside the immediate district which the library normally serves are refused, the librarian's work is unlikely to be much lessened as events make industrialists realise more and more how great a part education must play in research, management, workshop organisation and practice, and the technical processes of production.

Works libraries—by which is meant those formed for the use of scientific and technical research staffs as distinct from the library of text-books for the artisan—have been increasing in numbers and size during recent years, but they are still very uneven in quality. Those of large concerns engaged in the production of basic materials on which constant research is essential are so well stocked and administered that they occupy an honoured place among special libraries. Others are libraries in name only: many firms seem to think that a cupboard of books and a few periodicals, with a junior clerk or an unsuitable laboratory assistant to act as "librarian" by keeping a record of loans, are adequate for scientific and technical study. It seems clear that much educational work among industrialists is needed to make them realise how important a good works library is to their future; perhaps the fierce blast of competition will provide the stimulus.

COMMERCIAL AND TECHNICAL LIBRARIES

Projected developments in the provision of scientific and technical information may alter the type of demand made on the technical library by large firms with good library and information services, which will probably obtain more material direct from national sources; but the growth of the now immature libraries of other firms will fill the gap. If, as is hoped, their clerks are replaced in due course by trained librarians and information officers, this process will be accelerated. Moreover, even the smallest firms which could never aspire to a full-scale library may be stimulated to interest themselves in technical study and provide some periodicals. The commercial and technical librarian can be of real assistance to them, for they have no other skilled guide to books and information.

It seems likely then, that in the future the library's work with industry will change little in content, though it may increase in volume. Methods of recording the existence and nature of material of interest to local industry may have to be extended or varied as new enquiries are received from representatives of firms which hitherto have looked askance at any information culled from books or other printed matter. Much "information resistance" still remains to be overcome before advances in science and technology can percolate from research centres to many small businesses. Nevertheless, the use of the library by smaller firms will almost certainly increase. When the librarian tries to foster it, he will find that the sources available for general

THE FUTURE

technical information are not wholly satisfactory and may feel that the bodies concerned with the dissemination of scientific and technical information have perhaps laid too much stress on the research side.

Aids to industrial research

Abstracts are useful both to research workers and practising technicians. They are produced by many bodies, comprising research associations, government departments, societies, institutions, industries and technical publishers, but some branches of science and technology are still not covered. As so many different agencies do the work, they are uneven in scope and presentation and there is considerable overlapping.

One of the most important tasks of the works librarian or information officer is to compile and issue his own abstracts and other records of material likely to be useful in the research department and in shop practice. These must be prepared in accordance with the particular interests of his firm and the slant of research and production. Their selection includes regular searches for material and references among abstracts, patents, periodicals and other publications, often in consultation with the public technical librarian. Published abstracts are made in this country by experts in limited fields who are usually in touch with industrial needs and, in the case of the research associations, with colleagues undertaking research into problems often posed by industry itself. There is a danger—admittedly a small one—that this highly selective method of abstracting may lead to the occasional omission of important matter. On the other hand, it is obviously pointless to include the enormous output of periodical articles which are little more than technical hack journalism.

The organisation of an adequate national abstracting service is of such importance that it might well offer scope for a limited exercise of that current popular diversion known as "planning". The general principles under which abstracts are made and published in this country appear to be sound—though the possibility of the writer of a scientific article preparing and publishing his own abstract of it should certainly be examined[1]—but some authority should be created to lay down standards of production, to prevent overlapping, and to ensure an adequate coverage of subjects. An alternative is for a body, financed by the government, to undertake the work nationally on the lines of the Centre de Documentation du Centre National de la Recherche Scientifique sponsored by the French Ministry of Education, or the newly created Soviet Institute of Scientific Information, which is designed to produce abstracts for scientists from world literature on every aspect of science and technology. The Russian institute is already publishing monthly

---

[1] See Professor J. D. Bernal's suggestions for the international presentation of scientific information in "Information service as an essential in the progress of science". *ASLIB. Report of proceedings of the Twentieth Conference*, 1945, pp. 23-24.

THE FUTURE

abstract journals on mechanics, mathematics and astronomy, and a fortnightly one on chemistry, and is expected soon to add biology, geology and technology to the list.

If the suggested improvements can be made, the methods in use in this country seem preferable to a centralised national abstracting service. Unless a radically different plan is adopted, abstracts should continue to be published in subject groups, though it would be helpful if a cumulated general index to them could be compiled.

Consideration should also be given to the cumulative indexing of periodicals. The full scope of the *Engineering Index* makes it an indispensable tool to librarians, but the much narrower range of periodicals covered by the *Industrial Arts Index* and its American bias limit its usefulness in this country. A British index of scientific and technical periodicals, produced with the efficiency of the American ones, would be a most valuable contribution to the attempts now being made to bring the latest discoveries of scientists to the notice of the producers of goods, but it seems obvious that, as in the case of a full abstracting service, it could only be maintained by a governmental subsidy.

The amount of published matter on science and technology is growing at an almost terrifying rate; and the difficulties of finding among it particular items of value for specific purposes increase proportionately. It would be very helpful if, in the near future, methods could be devised to reduce the time now being spent on such searches all over the country which, in total, must be enormous.[1] Perhaps one of the electronic contrivances, which seem to be able to perform the most astonishing feats, could be used; certainly a close watch should be kept on the possibilities of these machines, and of new techniques in photographic and other processes. In this age of invention, no new device is too fanciful for consideration. For example, some interesting experiments in translating Russian scientific and technical articles by means of the machine popularly known as an "electronic brain" have been carried out in the United States.[2] The choice of scientific matter for these tests was deliberate; words used in it have very narrow meanings, and though grammar disappeared in mechanical translation, a reader with scientific training was able to understand the sense of the passages. The difficulties of translating so flexible a medium as language by mechanical means are obvious. Nevertheless, these experiments may presage future wonders which could be harnessed to the task of disseminating knowledge.

Problems of interest to public and industrial technical librarians and information officers have been under consideration by certain committees

---

[1] The extent to which developments of existing punched card systems can be harnessed to this task is shown in two articles in *Chemical and Engineering News:* "New tools for the resurrection of knowledge", Vol. 32, 1954, pp. 866–9, and "Information for sale", p. 966.

[2] *Chemical and Engineering News*, Vol. 32, 1954, pp. 340–341.

THE FUTURE

appointed by the government, and their recommendations are discussed below.

Proposed science centre

For many years the scientific societies have been pressing the government to establish a science centre in which the larger scientific societies could be suitably housed under one roof and their libraries pooled for the common use of their members. Some progress in negotiation was made after 1944, when the Lord President of the Council first received a deputation representing the societies. In 1950 the Royal Society was informed that the scheme had made great progress in that an adequate central site had been selected and that the Treasury had undertaken to provide the cost of building. Later, in the year it was stated in the House of Commons that suitable new quarters would be built for the Royal Society and other leading scientific societies and their libraries; that the Department of Scientific and Industrial Research and other government scientific organisations would also be housed there; and that provision would be made for the Patent Office and its library, which would be extended and modernised to serve as a central reference library in science and technology. The enlarged library will serve working scientists in industry and all concerned with research and technical development, but will not provide for other users, such as undergraduate students, who must use other existing facilities. A novel suggestion is that scientific literature more than about 50 years old shall be pruned in consultation with the British Museum.

These proposals would have been extended had the recommendations of the Report on Scientific and Technical Library Facilities prepared by the Panel on Technical Information Services of the Committee on Industrial Productivity been adopted. The Advisory Council on Scientific Policy dealt with them in their third report (July 1950) as follows:—

"The Panel reported that the development of technical library facilities had failed to keep pace with the growth of scientific research. While the money expended on research had greatly increased, the funds, accommodation and staff available to the scientific and technical libraries had, in general, remained static, and these libraries were no longer capable of maintaining full collections of technical literature, and of providing reasonable facilities for readers. Industrial and other users were therefore badly handicapped in keeping abreast of, and making use of, scientific results, on the obtaining of which much public money had been expended.

"The Panel recommended that, in order to secure effective and co-ordinated action, a Scientific and Technical Library Authority should be set up as a semi-independent agency of the Government to run central loan and reference libraries, and to advise and assist financially other technical libraries. Its first duty would be to develop a central reference library in London, if possible in close association with specialised libraries of the learned societies, and to develop a national lending library of science and technology, not necessarily in London. It was thought that the existing Patent Office Library might form the basis of the proposed central refer-

THE FUTURE

ence library, and that the existing library of the Science Museum might form the nucleus of the lending library. Better use of the scientific literature in the British Museum Library should also be facilitated, and the Authority should ensure an adequate supply of suitably trained personnel in the various technical libraries, and should support the provision of union catalogues, and the development of comprehensive scientific and technical sections in public libraries, particularly in the main industrial centres.

"It might also keep under review, and encourage the development of, new library techniques and mechanical aids which would assist in the creation of a more economic and efficient service."

The Advisory Council commented on the above as follows:—

"While agreeing with the diagnosis and broad objectives stated by the Panel, we felt doubtful whether the case for an executive Scientific and Technical Library Authority was made out. We consider that the objects which the Panel had in view could be achieved by existing organisations, given effective co-operation and increased support for their efforts. We therefore decided to constitute, with your approval, a Standing Scientific Library and Technical Information Committee of the Advisory Council on Scientific Policy:

(i) to co-ordinate the development of scientific libraries as a whole, and to consider in greater detail the parts to be played by individual libraries;
(ii) to examine their additional requirements in the light of the needs of users;
(iii) to review the recruitment and training of scientific librarians;

(iv) to initiate and co-ordinate the preparation of union lists; and

(v) to devise and introduce as soon as possible a system of common or interchangeable readers' tickets for those libraries where tickets are required.

"We consider that in this way co-ordination can readily be achieved by bringing those interested together, and that the necessary support for the provision or extension of facilities can be enlisted. In our view the necessary knowledge and organisations already exist but they urgently need increased resources and a higher status if they are to meet the national need."

It will be noted that the Advisory Council, in framing the terms of reference of the new Standing Scientific Library and Technical Information Committee it proposed to set up, omitted the proposal for a national lending library of science and technology and the special reference to the development of scientific and technical collections in public libraries.

A National Lending Library of Science and Technology

The fifth and sixth annual reports of the Advisory Council make no further mention of the proposal to create a National Lending Library of Science and Technology, one of the most important and practical recommendations of the Panel on Technical Information Services. It may be that this, and other matters, are still under consideration, or that external loans are contemplated from the proposed National Reference Library of Science

THE FUTURE

and Technology, though this would hardly be in keeping with its purpose.

While there will probably be general support for the proposal to create the National Reference Library—though librarians may reflect that the inhabitants of London are fortunate in having so many library facilities provided for them out of national funds while forty million other people in Britain have to make shift as best they can—technical librarians may feel that the provision of a more adequate loan service of scientific and technical literature is of equal, if not greater, importance. The Science Museum Library is invaluable to them and to industrial research libraries; indeed, the success of its work has created demands which it is increasingly unable to satisfy by its existing resources. Apart from the considerable amount of material in the "No-loan" list, important sources are sometimes not available without long delays because they have already been lent or are being bound. Duplicacation of frequently needed material is therefore clearly desirable. If, as can be anticipated, greater interest in scientific and technical research is aroused among industrialists, the calls on this library are likely to grow to an extent that will make its expansion an urgent national necessity.

Librarians have an amiable weakness for devising grandiose schemes for national book coverage which bear so little relation to reality that they have small chance of acceptance by reponsible national bodies. Such a plan was published in 1949 as an interim report of the Library Association.[1] So far as its main principles can be seen through the thicket of jargon surrounding them, it is proposed to cover the needs of every type of book user by creating an elaborate and gradated series of libraries whose functions and work will be linked up in some way as yet unspecified. It may be that in due course the efforts of educationalists and librarians, or even the pressure of economic necessity, will result in a considerable proportion of the population asking for books on a scale quite unimaginable now; but there are few signs of this happening, nor, in the opinion of many qualified to judge, is it ever likely to do so to an extent that would justify such extravagant schemes. The number of people who need special literature for humane or scientific studies from sources not readily available is never likely to be very large. Most of them require it during their university training, when the university libraries, aided by their own interloan scheme, adequately cater for them; the number of those who continue their studies once they have obtained the passport to some standard of economic security is distressingly small; working specialists have access to many library sources; and it is probable that the wants of the remaining advanced readers or research workers could be satisfied by much simpler, more effective and less costly machinery than that

[1] "The co-operative provision of books, periodicals and related material: an interim report". *Library Association Record*, 1949, pp. 383–387.

suggested in the report. Second thoughts are usually better than the somewhat uncritical enthusiasms of the first ones, and it is noted that in the second interim report[1] a much more modest and sensible contribution to the problem is suggested.

It is outside the scope of this work to deal with the larger aspect of co-operative book provision in the immense literature concerned with humane studies, but it would be invidious if, in discussing the most suitable means of serving scientific and technical workers, no mention were made of the work of the National Central Library and its outliers, or the efforts of librarians to provide, through the regional schemes, books for all who have real need of them. Despite the limitations inherent in so loosely built an organisation with such large aims, it has been reasonably effective for general purposes and for much scientific and technical literature as well; but the length of time needed before requests can be satisfied restricts its usefulness in supplying material in response to urgent enquiries from technical libraries.

So far as scientific and technical literature is concerned, one well-equipped national lending library will be a more effective aid to other libraries than a number of "regional" lending libraries based on arbitrary geographical divisions. Administration of book loans would be simpler when only one

[1] "The co-operative provision of books, periodicals and related materials: second interim report." *Library Association Record*, 1954, pp. 16–17.

catalogue is needed, bibliographical errors in requests could be more easily corrected, and the inevitable delays of any postal interchange scheme based on a number of co-operating libraries would be eliminated. Provided that books and periodicals in known demand are heavily duplicated, the national lending library could probably supply most calls within three days of the request being posted, and in urgent cases even this could be reduced by using the telephone.

As a large proportion of the loans will be made by post, the library should be easily accessible to the postal services and railways. The greatest possible number of users should be able to collect their books from it direct, as this would save their own and the staff's time, since packing would be unnecessary in their case. Sentiment argues that as London already has many State aided or State provided libraries, the national lending library should be placed elsewhere; but the proper approach to this question surely is the practical one of deciding where the largest number of borrowers of scientific and technical material will be convenienced. Total population within a given area may not be a sure guide, and if such a library is founded it is hoped that conclusive tests will be made before its location is finally decided.

The national lending library should, however, be relieved of some of the pressure on its services for material of a less highly specialised kind by a corresponding expansion of the resources and responsibilities of existing public technical libraries, each

THE FUTURE

of which already practises a form of subject specialisation. It would be helped if all the technical libraries in the industrial centres formed area interchange schemes. This is an immediate and practical measure and only a simple organisation is needed to make it effective if its work is confined to the pooling of published matter; it would, in addition, help firms near to public technical libraries to obtain material quickly. But as it is desirable under existing conditions to set a limit to the distance over which such interchange schemes operate, so that urgently wanted material already on loan can be returned by car within a short time, any great increase of book loans and the distances they are sent could only be made if the stocks and staffs of the technical libraries are strengthened. They would then face, though on a much smaller scale, precisely the same problems as the national lending library, and any additional services they accept should rank for government grants. It is obviously unfair to expect the large local authorities, which have already provided the libraries, to shoulder further financial burdens, and so far no one seems to have devised a method of levying contributions towards the cost of interchange schemes which would have a proper relation to services rendered.

It is usually wiser to expand existing services than to create new ones. Each established public technical library is already serving an industrial area; between them, they probably cover the major needs of industry throughout the country outside

COMMERCIAL AND TECHNICAL LIBRARIES

London, which is in a special position. Given financial support, and linked with other institutional and works libraries by interchange schemes, they could extend their services on a sensible and practical plan so as to include rural industries within their orbit. The main industrial areas, which surround the large towns, are not evenly distributed geographically, and some industries would be left outside the scheme; but they would be relatively so few that their demands on the national lending library would probably be more than counterbalanced by the relief obtained if the public technical libraries were developed in the way suggested.

Technical information services—the F.B.I. Report

In collaboration with the Panel on Technical Information Services, the Federation of British Industries made an enquiry "into the part that local municipal libraries do play, or ought to play, in providing a technical information service to industry". A questionnaire was distributed to a proportion of firms in membership, but the questions were so unhappily framed that they were unlikely to elicit the real facts.

It is therefore not surprising that the results of this enquiry gave no support to any serious claims which may have been made on behalf of public library information services to industry. Only one library, with an already excellent reputation in this field, received full marks in that the five firms which replied praised its work in the warmest terms; another

THE FUTURE

received three commendatory notices. In general, however, the report makes it clear that industry as a whole makes little use of public library facilities throughout the country. The most obvious reason is that they do not provide the books needed, but some replies seem to show that many engaged in industry have little knowledge of the work public libraries do or the way in which the different services are organised, because many criticisms are on points of detail which could easily be altered. Some intelligent "public relations" activity in industry seems to be required of public librarians.

The report probably influenced the attitude to public libraries of the committees concerned. This is unfortunate, because it is not easy to ascertain the real facts by an enquiry conducted in this way. The matter is of such importance that it clearly calls for a survey planned on more scientific lines, which would differentiate between libraries with special technical services and those without them and deal more precisely with the details of such services. No one reading the report without knowledge of the work of public technical libraries could possibly believe that some of them provide efficient technical information services and a wide range of scientific and technical literature to large numbers of firms.

Technical information services—the Panel on Technical Information Services Report
The Report of the Panel on Technical Informa-

tion Services of the Committee on Industrial Productivity[1] is an important document which has been passed by the Advisory Council on Scientific Policy to its Standing Scientific Library and Technical Information Committee "in order that the Panel's recommendations may be examined with a view to implementation".[2] The report under review here deals with technical information services and should not be confused with a previous report of the Panel on library provision mentioned earlier in this chapter.

As stated in one of the introductory paragraphs, "it is particularly concerned with the setting-up of special bureaux and advisory services, and the appointment of technical information officers and industrial liaison officers in public or non-profit making organisations such as Government Departments or Research Associations. Other forms of technical information, such as publication in scientific journals, abstract publications, the provision of libraries, the services of the technical press, and industrial consultant services, are not discussed in detail".

The report is a well-reasoned and clear presentation of the Panel's case and the whole should be read; here it is only possible to summarise the parts of particular interest to public technical librarians, though the three paragraphs referring specifically to public libraries are quoted in full. The summary

[1] Published in the *Journal of Documentation*, Vol. 7, 1951, pp. 92–112.
[2] *Fourth Annual Report of the Advisory Council on Scientific Policy* (1950–51), p. 11.

THE FUTURE

includes as far as possible the actual words used in the report.

Summary of the report on technical information services

Existing research institutions specialising in particular fields of applied science which receive numerous enquiries from industry should appoint information and industrial liaison officers if they have not already done so. The information officers should filter the growing number of enquiries directed to the institutions so that the time of the research scientist will not be wasted on comparatively trivial matters. One of the most important functions of the information officer is, in fact, to protect his research colleagues. The industrial liaison officer, who is in daily contact with industry and works with his research colleagues and has easy access to recorded information, can provide practical guidance to an external enquirer and keep his colleagues in touch with industrial practice. He should also be able to awaken the interest of the heads of smaller firms in new developments.

As certain subjects are not covered by technical information services which make information generally available, the Department of Scientific and Industrial Research (D.S.I.R.) should make a survey of the gaps in the coverage. In the meantime, until provision has been made for them, D.S.I.R. Headquarters Intelligence Division should deal with any questions from small firms unable to undertake their own research and other information services should be asked to co-operate.

As at present there is no recognised procedure for deciding where to send enquiries and many are directed to inappropriate organisations, residual enquiries for which there is no obvious channel should either be dealt with by D.S.I.R. Headquarters Information Service, or where necessary directed by it to the best sources of information.

COMMERCIAL AND TECHNICAL LIBRARIES

Small firms not in membership of a research association might best be given help in the application of the results of research on a regional basis by developing the activities of certain regional bodies interested in such matters, to which "field engineers" (on the Canadian plan) might well be attached.

International exchange of technical information should be encouraged in every possible way, but questions addressed to other countries should be confined to those which cannot fully be answered at home.

Abstracts, though mainly used by advanced firms, are so generally useful that newly established information groups are recommended to prepare them for subjects not already covered.

The maximum use should be made of information compiled by supply and service departments consonant with national security. D.S.I.R. might be given authority to survey such material and recommend de-classification of publications of value to industry on the lines of the United States Office of Technical Services.

The position of public libraries in the information system

"As already stated there is in this country no generally recognized procedure for routing inquiries. In the case of laboratories and firms possessing technically qualified staff, direct approach will normally be made to the relevant research association, government station, or to D.S.I.R. In other instances visits from an industrial liaison officer may be the origin of the questions. In still other instances approach may be made to public libraries or those of professional or learned societies.

"A recent survey made by us showed that taking the country as a whole industrial organizations make very little direct use of public libraries. Nevertheless these libraries

THE FUTURE

have a potential value in this connexion, since 600 library authorities in the country maintain in every town and village a service which is used by 12 million readers. Some of the libraries, especially those in the main industrial centres, hold considerable amounts of technical literature and can offer some guidance to more specialized sources of information; in some instances they are widely used.

"It is considered that the public libraries should be encouraged to improve their service on technical matters and their holdings of technical literature; in particular, the following steps might be taken:

(1) assistance might be given to libraries to help them to decide what technical books to acquire or retain;
(2) some technically trained staff might be acquired by libraries in the more important industrial centres;
(3) the libraries might be supplied with guides to the scope of more specialist organizations and with directions as to how the more technical inquiries should be forwarded."

The Panel's analysis of the position and their recommendations are generally reasonable and sound, but it is disappointing to find that work which technical libraries have been doing with some success for over thirty years has apparently not been recognised. The paragraphs relating to public libraries, though perhaps appropriate to those which have no special provision for scientific and technical information, can hardly be applied to technical libraries with a record of outstanding and pioneer work. Their librarians will no doubt be suitably gratified, for instance, to learn that they "can offer some guidance to more specialised sources

COMMERCIAL AND TECHNICAL LIBRARIES

of information". It is regrettable that in a national scheme for the provision of technical information for industry no suitable place can be found for institutions which have remarkable experience in this field and offer unique opportunities for further rewarding activities.

It seems that the Panel were impressed by the Federation of British Industries report which, as has already been pointed out, did not offer a suitable basis for any conclusions about the information services of technical libraries. Had a direct question about this been included, there can be little doubt that firms in the larger centres would have been glad to mention the many occasions when they have been given adequate replies to questions of importance to research and production. It is unfortunate, too, that the Panel lacked the advice of a public librarian with wide experience of special technical libraries and their relations with industry.

It would be absurd to make extravagant claims for public technical libraries, particularly in regard to research. Their limitations are well known; some have been mentioned earlier in this chapter. Compared with the holdings of the Science Museum, their periodical files are small[1] and the number

[1] "... [The Science Museum Library] ... which, according to the World List contains some six times as many titles in the scientific and technical periodical field as that of all the public libraries in the country put together . . ." (Urquhart, D. J. "Public libraries and industry." D.S.I.R., 1953, p. 5.) Though the general conclusion is valid, this statement is rather misleading since each library is bound to provide a large number of well-known periodicals stocked in the others.

THE FUTURE

of their books limited. Nevertheless, they could make some valuable contributions to an organised scheme for technical information services which are surely worthy of consideration. They were created because there was a need for them; their services have developed naturally as the demands of industry for information have increased and the range of research and invention has widened; their staffs have acquired a useful knowledge of the industries of the area they serve; and they have devised and practised methods of service, both personal and technical, of great value to their industrial users. Libraries whose activities have built up helpful relations with industry have at their disposal the knowledge and advice of experts in many fields—experts whose work is finally tested by that most effective of all criteria, the production plan. Some have gained the goodwill of industry to a remarkable degree. The extent to which good personal relationships between the staff and industry allow a regular flow of knowledge and experience between them can only be appreciated by those familiar with such activities. The telephones are in constant use for question and answer, check and countercheck of material and ideas, and for requests from the librarian to his colleagues in industry for advice in dealing with aspects of production, often carried out by small firms, about which sometimes the only available information is in the minds of those who make the article.

Good library service largely depends on the right contacts being made between readers and the librarian, and paper schemes for national coverage of books and information lose much of their value when they fail to give adequate weight to this basic fact. The value of public technical libraries rests on a solid foundation of confidence between them and their users. Their services could be extended if financial help were forthcoming from national sources, for it is hardly likely that, with the upward trend in rates, public libraries will be able to provide additional funds for activities which now reach out far beyond the boundaries of their authorities. That a service which has already proved its worth in the industrial areas should be virtually ignored at a time when millions of pounds are being spent from national and counterpart funds[1] to further industrial productivity would be unthinkable were it not apparent that public technical libraries seem to have been judged, not by what the best have done and are doing, but by what the worst have failed to do. The findings of the Federation of British Industries inquiry are hardly creditable to public libraries as a whole; but since one technical library emerged from this not particularly appropriate test with credit, would it not be reasonable to believe that with adequate funds and suitable guidance, others could do so also?

It might be helpful to describe the actual working of the information service of a progressive technical

[1] Arrangements for the expenditure of counterpart funds derived from United States economic aid (Cmd. 8776), and Programmes of expenditure of counterpart funds derived from United States economic aid (Cmd. 8918). H.M.S.O. 1953.

THE FUTURE

library which is the centre of a closely knit industrial area. The information officers of industrial research and development departments naturally submit specialist enquiries concerned with their products, which their own experts cannot answer, direct to the research associations or the government research departments, which give them excellent service. They know that the public technical library, though its holdings in general and special material are extensive, is not likely to be able to help them with such enquiries; but questions relating to other subjects are usually first tested in it either for actual information or for sources which may help to answer them. All are subject to the time factor. If an enquiry relates to a production process which may be held up at heavy cost to the firm, the answer is wanted immediately; if, on the other hand, it is concerned with research on a long term project, it must be at hand within a fixed time for consideration at the regular meetings of the research and production experts working on it. ASLIB Information Service is useful as a guide to sources; the Department of Scientific and Industrial Research Headquarters, which is mainly a routing agency, generally farms out the kind of question posed by such firms, with the result that answers are sometimes considerably delayed.

Very few firms have established really good libraries with trained librarians and competent information officers, though they may have well-equipped research facilities. It might be assumed that those which have done so will make few calls on the services the public technical library can offer. In actual fact they use them extensively. Their information officers send in advance regular (sometimes daily) lists of wants and often devote one day each week to personal visits to check current publications or to pursue enquiries with the aid of the staff. The library's wide coverage of subjects enables them to use it for information about finished products of which the material under research is designed ultimately to become a part; and many aspects of study perhaps only distantly connected with matters under examination in the laboratories are dealt with in its stock. It is a suggestive fact that the firms with the best libraries and information services use the technical library most.

Industrial information officers, helped by their expert colleagues, are able to submit complex questions to research organisations in clear and precise terms; but the technical library deals each year with thousands of enquiries from firms which, having no libraries or information officers, are unable or unwilling to do so. Many of them manufacture a limited range of special products and their enquiries are therefore often confidential. For this reason, questions are sometimes put so indirectly that the librarian has difficulty in finding out their real nature; indeed, it is only when the firm has confidence in his judgment and discretion that the enquiries can be clarified by frank discussion. In such cases the librarian himself must be equally

THE FUTURE

discreet in asking other firms for advice or information which may help him to produce a satisfactory answer to the question originally posed. Apart from the important matter of secrecy, many enquiries by smaller firms can only be resolved after frequent personal or telephonic consultations during the process of search. The librarian naturally goes beyond his own resources for answers he himself is unable to provide. It is surely wishful thinking to imagine that such enquiries are likely to be directed to remote research bodies or that they can be so clearly presented in written form as to elicit a correct reply.

It will be seen that the public technical librarian is, in fact, carrying out the "screening" duties so properly allotted to the information officers attached to the research bodies; but he is in a better position than they to deal with many questions because of his local knowledge and his personal relations with the "consumer of technical intelligence". Consumer interest is paramount, but apart from a few large firms which have built up their own information services, the main body of actual and potential industrial users of information only have access to it by correspondence unless they use a technical library. It is astonishing and disturbing that this most important point of contact should not have been given a suitable part in the proposed set-up.

The fact that many firms are not members of research organisations is recognised in the report and it is proposed to help them in two ways: (1)

by the appointment of regional industrial liaison officers, who will be able to follow up an enquiry by giving technical advice and who will be based on such bodies as the Manchester Joint Research Council, the Midland Council for Productivity, or the Scottish Council for Development in Industry, and (2) by a publicity campaign to inform them of the purposes of the national technical information system.

The principles may be right, but the value of the proposed application of them seems debatable. It is not easy to see what advantages are likely to be gained by attaching industrial liaison officers to general bodies like those mentioned, which, being regional rather than local, must cover a great range of industrial practices. On the other hand, the industrial areas grouped around the cities with technical libraries have such clearly defined and closely integrated interests that it would have seemed wiser to base the scheme on these natural groupings, possibly under the auspices of Area Industrial Productivity Committees. At the heart of the area is the public technical library, which would provide an excellent base of operations for the industrial liaison officer, for it already has regular contacts with many of his potential clients and, in addition, generally offers the same conditions as are held to be so important to the duties of similar officers of the research associations.

If enlarged and strengthened by the grant of even a fraction of the sums now being so lavishly

THE FUTURE

distributed, the technical library would be better equipped, through its extensive industrial contacts and its experience of area industries, to make known and operate some of the facilities for technical information services it is proposed to provide. It could, of course, distribute the brochures and other publications on which considerable sums from counterpart funds are to be spent, and they might be more effective if this were done personally by the librarian when he is dealing with the thousands of enquiries directed to him. Public librarians, who have been much used as propaganda agencies, hardly share the general assumption that the printed word carries conviction to minds unprepared to receive its message. It is scarcely likely to do so among the owners of small industrial establishments who tend to believe that the industrial life of Britain revolves around their particular product. As has been stated earlier in this work, librarians know from experience how hard it is to find a chink in the armour of self-satisfaction in which the owner of a small family business or the worker who has created an industrial niche encases himself. If the librarian who knows his people is unable to pierce it, printed explanations and exhortations, however attractively produced, are unlikely to do so.

There is little point in examining more closely the Panel's general recommendations about public libraries. Apart from special technical libraries, it is unfortunately true that the book stocks of many are of little use to industry or to students, and the danger of keeping on the shelves books long outdated is particularly applicable to these subjects. It is to be hoped that the Standing Scientific Library and Technical Information Committee will at least advocate grants to enable public libraries to build up their stocks of scientific and technical books; for however well planned and effective the provision for research and information services may become, for the great majority of technicians, students and industrial workers in general, the public library will probably remain the only easily accessible source of suitable literature.

THE END

INDEX

Abstracts, made in industrial establishments, 283; of patents, 182; proposed national abstracting service, 284-5; selection of, 150-1, 163; Soviet Institute of Scientific Information, 284-5
Adams, Robert, 27-8
Adaptive planning, 80
Addresses, cable, index of, 228
Administration, departmental independence, 195-7; public service, 201-3; reference or partly home reading library, 192-4
Advisory Council on Scientific Policy, reports, 288-90
Annuals, selection of, 130-2
Associations, commercial, index of, 228
Atomic energy reports, deposit libraries, 163-4; publicity for, 247

Bibliographies, for individual readers, 232-3; preparation (for classes), 253-4; printed, 257; research, 255-7; —exchanges with other organisations, 256; supply of bulk copies, 254-5, supply to classes, etc., 253-5
Birmingham, Commercial Library, 52, 65; Technical Library, 52, 65
Books, displays, 245-6; duplication in home reading libraries, 276; loan of, 204; local union catalogue (Interchange Scheme), 262; misplacement on shelves, 204; on pure science, inclusion of, 152-4; shelf register, 212-4; theft of, 205
Book selection, commercial library, 126-49; dependence on policy decisions, 125-6; technical library, 149-64; use of bibliographies, 164-7

Book stack, 79-80
Bristol Commercial Library, 52, 65
Bulletins, 257-8

Catalogue, classified or dictionary, 208-9; form of, 211-2; local union catalogue (Interchange Scheme), 262; stand, 98
Cataloguing methods, 209-11
Chairs, 92
Chamber of Commerce, collaboration with, 248
Classification, 206-8
Clippings file, 226
Codes, telegraphic, selection of, 132-4
Colleges of Commerce, Science and Technology, collaboration with, 277-80; help of staff in book selection, 249; training pupils in use of books, 251-3, 278-80
Commercial associations, index of, 228
Commercial federations, index of, 228
Commercial law cases reports, index of, 228
Commercial library, book selection, 126-49; future development, 274
Commodities, index of, 228
Consuls, contact with, 247-8
Co-operative Information and Commercial Reference Information Service (CICRIS), 267-8
Copying, microfilm and photocopy, 78
Correspondence, 197-8
Counter, staff service, 98-100
Coventry, Commercial Library, 51; Technical Library, 52

Dictionaries, multi-lingual, 149

311

INDEX

Directories, arrangement, 222-3; public index of, 223-4; selection of, 128-32; shelving, 87-8
Directories and codes, circulating lists of, 246-7
Discarding, 168-9
Display fittings, 88-91
Displays of books, 245-6
Dundee Commercial Library, 52

Edinburgh Commercial Library, 52
Education, in use of library, 250-3; scientific and technological—effect on public libraries, 269-80
Educational institutions, collaboration with, 277-80; supply of bibliographies to, 253-5
Electronic contrivances, use in research, 286
Enclosure, staff, 98-100
Enquiries, limits to be set, 231-2; personal and telephonic, 229-32; record of, 230
Establishment of commercial and technical libraries, conditions affecting, 55-66; effect of existence of other libraries, 57-9; needs of surrounding area, 59-60; reasons why needed, 62-5; type of library, 65-6
Exhibitions, use of, 243-5

Federation of British Industries, report on public libraries, 296-7, 302
Federations, commercial, index of, 228
Formation of commercial and technical libraries. *See* Establishment.

Geographical names, index of, 227
Glasgow Commercial Library, 27, 28-9, 54, 65
Government publications, 156-8

Holborn Commercial Library, 54, 56
Hours of opening, 203

Hull Commercial and Technical Library, 54

Indexes, special, 225-9
Industrial firms, supply of bibliographies to, 255-6
Industrialists, difficulties of attracting to library, 235-6
Industrial liaison officers, based on public technical libraries, 307-9
Industrial research establishments, relations with, 280-3; supply of bibliographies to, 255-6
Information, general, index of, 226-7
Information officers, training of, 118-20
Interchange Scheme, 258-66; benefits to public library, 266-7; conditions of membership, 262-3; extension of range, 264-5
Issue methods, 214-6; records, 214-6; —exceptions to, 215-6

Leeds Commercial and Technical Library, 51, 65-6
Leicester Commercial and Technical Library, 52
Liaison officers, industrial, based on public technical libraries, 307-9
Librarian, degree of independence allowed, 195-7; personal contacts, 196-7
Library Association, report on co-operative provision of books, 291-3 Technical and Commercial Libraries Special Committee, 32, 33-6, 38, 43-4, 50-1
Lighting, artificial, 82-5; cathode, 84-5 natural, 75, 82; table, 92
Lists, study and reading. *See* Bibliographies.
Liverpool, Commercial Library, 31, 65; Technical Library, 54, 65
Loan of books, for home reading 192-4; for industrial use, 204

INDEX

Location, in main building, 78-9; in town, 66-70

London, City of, proposed Mercantile Library, 19;—commercial collection, 21, 56;—list of directories, 129; co-operative information service (CICRIS), 267-8

Manchester, Commercial Library, 52-3, 65; Technical Library, 52-3, 65

Map fittings, 96-8

Maps, selection of, 135-6; table for use of, 92

Markets and prices reports, index of, 228

Modular planning, 80

National Lending Library of Science and Technology, location of, 294; proposal for establishment, 288, 290-6; supplementing service of, 294-6

National plan for access to scientific and technological literature and information, 269-310

National Reference Library of Science and Technology, proposal for establishment, 287-9, 291

Newcastle-upon-Tyne Commercial and Technical Library, 54

Newspapers, selection of, 171-2

Patent Office Library, indexes to patents, 178; proposed development of, 287-9

Patents, abridgements, 176-7; abstracts of, 182; arrears in publication of, 174-7; Commonwealth and foreign, location of, 182-8; deposit libraries, 173; —publicity for, 247; details of publications, 175-9; indexes, difficulties in using, 177-8; —in Patent Office Library, 178; —microfilm of, 178; methods of filing, 180-2; photocopying, 179; punched card system for searchers (Patent Office), 179-80;

types of enquiries received, 177; United States specifications, 173, 182-8

Periodical indexes, need for British, 285; selection of, 150

Periodicals, arrangement, 218-9; filing, 220-2; fittings for, 92-6; gifts of, 217; printed indexes, 150; public index to, 219-20; receipt of, 217; selection of, 169-71; supplementary staff index to technical, 228-9; theft of, 218; union list of local holdings (Interchange Scheme), 261; use of cases for, 96

Personal contacts of librarian, 247-9

Planning, adaptive, 80; book store, 77; general conditions affecting, 72-4; modular, 80; position of department in main building, 78-9; size of room, 74; sound proof rooms, 78; staff working space, 76-7; staff workrooms, 81-2

Plans of towns, docks, etc., 136

Prices and markets reports, index of, 228

Professional classes, difficulties of attracting to library, 235-6

Professional societies, supply of bibliographies to, 255

Publications, sponsored, 159-60

Publicity, caution needed in use of, 237; general, 237-43; importance of written word, 237-8; in books, 242; in newspapers, 241-2, 243; limitations of, 239-40; need for, 234; newspaper advertisements, 243; posters, 243; principles governing, 238-9; specially directed, 246-7; use of existing publications, 240-1

Public library, place in national plan, 269; reasons for neglect of, 270-3

Public relations, personal contacts, 247-9

Public service, 201-3

Readers, control of, 205-6; difficulties

313

INDEX

of attracting, 235-6; possible future increase in numbers of, 273-7; unsatisfactory, 206

Reading lists. *See* Bibliographies.

Reference libraries in branches, 277

Reference or partly home reading library, 192-4

Regional lending libraries, comments on, 293-6

Replacements, 167-8

Research, bibliographies, 256-7; changed conditions of, 60-1; —effect on public library, 61-2; establishments, future relations with, 280-3; —Interchange Scheme, 258-66

Savage, E. A., 31, 33, 40, 46, 49

School pupils, diversion to other libraries, 275-7; possible increased use of library by, 273-7; training in the use of books, 250-1

Science and Technology, proposed National Lending Library of, 288, 290-6; proposed National Reference Library of, 287-9, 291

Science Centre, proposed, 287-90

Science Library, Science Museum, proposed development of, 289; United States atomic energy reports deposited, 163; value of, 291

Scientific and technological literature, need for grants, 310; possible increase in readers of, 273-7

Scientific and technological literature and information, national plans for access to, 269-310; —disabilities of public libraries, 270-2

Secondary school pupils, diversion to other libraries, 275-7; training in the use of books, 250-1

Service, public, 201-3

Services, need to advertise, 234

Sheffield, Commercial and Technical Library, 52-3, 65-6; United States, British and Canadian atomic energy reports deposited, 163-4

Shelf register, 212-4

Shelves, checking book order on, 204-5

Shelving, adjustable or fixed, 86-7; directory, 87-8; raked, 86; wall, 74-5; wooden or metal, 85-6

Societies, publications of, 159; visits of, 250

Southwark Commercial Library, 52, 56

Specifications, patents, 173-88; standards, 160-1

Sponsored publications, 159-60

Standard specifications, 160-1

Staff, background knowledge, 110-5; conditions affecting selection of, 101-16; mental qualities and aptitudes, 109-10; men or women, 115-6 natural aptitudes, 121-4; personal qualities, 108-9; science graduates, 114-5; scientific education, 113-4; standard of education, 110-5; standards of service, 201-3; working space, 76-7; workrooms, 81-2

Staff training, accuracy, 199-200; in administration, 198-200; library technique, 105-7; practical training, 120-4; theoretical, 116-20

Statistics, index of publications, containing, 227-8

Stock records, 212-4

Students, advanced, training in the use of books, 278-80

Study lists. *See* Bibliographies.

Subjects, selection of, for commercial library, 139-49; for technical library, 151-6

Table lighting, 92

Tables, choice of, 91-2; for use of maps, 92

Tariffs, index of, 228

Technical Information Services, Panel on, comments on public libraries, 300-1; recommendations on technical library facilities, 288-90; report

INDEX

on technical library facilities, 298-301; —criticism of, 301-9
Technical libraries, public future developments, 275-83; place in national plan, 301-9; service as area libraries, 294-6; working of information service, 304-7
Technical library, inclusion of books on pure science, 152-4; selection of subjects for, 151-6
Telephone, enquiries, 229-30; use of, 230
Telegraphic codes, selection of, 132-4
Time tables, selection of, 134-5
Trade catalogues, arrangement, 224-5; index of, 224-5; selection of, 135
Trade marks, applications for registration of, 189; directories containing, 223-4; index of, 191; librarian's help to intending applicants for registration, 189-91; publications listing, 190-1

Trades Technical Societies, supply of bibliographies to, 253
Translations, by mechanical means, 286; selection of, 161-3
Translators, index of local, 228

Unions, commercial, index of, 228
University, Extra-Mural Department classes, supply of bibliographies to, 253; library, collaboration with, 249; staff, help in book selection, 249

Westminster, commercial collection, 56; list of directories, etc., 129
Whisky money, 24-5
Wolverhampton Commercial Library, 52
Workrooms, staff, 81-2
Works libraries, Interchange Scheme, 258-66; relations with, 281-3

For Product Safety Concerns and Information please contact our EU representative GPSR@taylorandfrancis.com
Taylor & Francis Verlag GmbH, Kaufingerstraße 24, 80331 München, Germany

www.ingramcontent.com/pod-product-compliance
Lightning Source LLC
Chambersburg PA
CBHW071155300426
44113CB00009B/1220